BIBLE LESSONS FOR JUNIORS

BOOK 2
Kings and Prophets

Andrew Van Der Veer

FREE REFORMED PUBLICATIONS
and
REFORMATION HERITAGE BOOKS

Copyright © 1951 by
Baker Book House

Published in 2007 by

Free Reformed Publications
265 King George Road, Suite 104
Brantford, ON N3R 7Z9
CANADA
519-752-4413/ Fax: 519-751-4470
e-mail: publications@frcna.org

and

Reformation Heritage Books
2965 Leonard St., NE
Grand Rapids, MI 49525
USA
616-977-0599 / Fax 616-285-3246
e-mail: orders@heritagebooks.org
website: www.heritagebooks.org

ISBN #978-1-60178-013-3 (vol. 2)
978-1-60178-016-4 (set)

2nd printing 2013

Permission to reprint granted by Baker Book House

New cover design by Pronk Graphics

For additional Reformed literature, both new and used, request a
free book list from Reformation Heritage Books at the above address.

PREFACE

The Bible Lessons for Juniors is a series of four books designed to acquaint the junior child (ages 9 through 12) with the glad tidings of salvation as made known to us in God's Holy Word, the Bible.

Book 1 and Book 2 each contain 28 lessons on the Old Testament.
Book 3 contains 28 lessons on the four Gospels.
Book 4 contains 28 lessons on the Book of Acts.

SUGGESTIONS FOR THE USE OF THE SERIES

For the Student

The purpose of the Bible Lessons for Juniors series is to approach boys and girls in a very simple way with the main stories of the Bible. This series is written in their language and their experiences in their young life. This is no exhaustive study of the Bible, but includes the stories every junior-age boy or girl ought to know.

The series aims to direct boys and girls to the Bible, the Holy Scriptures. The Bible is quoted freely so as to accustom the learner to Bible language. The Scripture references require that the student use the Bible as the source book of study. Every junior age boy or girl should own a Bible.

The questions and answers are not intended to be memorized by rote, but are designed for the teacher and the students to review the lesson as a tool to reinforce Bible content. All the learning activities are designed to reinforce the Bible lesson and stimulate interest in Bible study.

The memory verse requires work from the student. Bible verses memorized in youth will stay with them for the rest of their lives.

For the Parents

The use of the series provides the parents with a helpful guide in studying the Bible with their children. It is suggested that parents so arrange their family worship that the Bible reference for the lessons be used at mealtime or for devotional purposes. This will make the Bible reading more systematic and help the whole family become more interested in Bible study.

For the Teacher

The lesson story is designed to give the teacher a guide. He or she should be well acquainted with the lesson material to give added detail to the story as much as reason and time will allow.

Older children can read the story themselves and the teacher can use the questions and answers to ensure students have studied the lesson at home. Scripture verses for memorization are chosen to be meaningful in relation to the lesson, as well as applicable to the lives of the boys and girls.

Personal Application

Those who have used the lessons have noted that the Bible stories have little or no personal application. This method focuses on the content of the Bible and ensures that the material can be used in every kind of church setting, no matter what the background of the children being taught.

The simple but truthful narration of the Bible stories allows the teacher to add his/her own personal application and comments, rather than deal with subjective views of the author. This lesson series is therefore a useful tool in the church, but also in an interdenominational or outreach setting.

Something to Think About

For the purpose of personal application there are questions, comments and thoughts on each lesson. These are intended to help the students to think for themselves about the implicit application of each Bible story for their lives. These thoughts may be somewhat advanced for the younger students, but we have tried to keep in mind the older children also. The teacher should feel free to offer his own thoughts and ask for such from the students.

It is our sincere prayer that this series may be of real service in guiding many into the blessed truth as it is in Christ Jesus. May it prepare them to know and confess Jesus Christ as their Saviour and Lord.

— Adapted from Andrew Van Der Veer
by Frederika Pronk, October 2006

Lesson 1

JOB, THE PATIENT BELIEVER

Read: Job 1, 2, 38-42

Before we continue our study of the Israelites, God's chosen people, we want to study the life of a God-fearing man named Job. We do not know exactly at what time Job lived. The Bible does tell us that he lived in the land of Uz.

Job was an upright man. He hated sin. This God-fearing man had seven sons and three daughters. He was a very rich man. He could count his sheep and camels by the thousands, and had many oxen and donkeys. He had many servants to do his work.

Job was very thoughtful about his children. Whenever his sons had a feast in their homes they would invite their sisters to party with them. Then Job would rise up early the next morning and offer sacrifices for them all. Job said "It may be that my sons have sinned." Job did not want anything to stand between God and his children.

It happened one day that the angels of God stood before the Lord. Satan, the evil one, came also and stood among them. The Lord said to Satan, "Whence comest thou?" Satan answered, "From going to and fro in the earth, and from walking up and down in it."

The Lord said to Satan, "Hast thou considered my servant Job, that there is none like him in the earth, a perfect and an upright man, one that feareth God and escheweth evil?"

Then Satan told God that Job feared the Lord because God had always blessed Job and his work. "But," said Satan, "put forth thine hand now, and touch all that he hath, and he will curse thee to thy face."

The Lord said to Satan, "Behold all that he hath is in thy power, only upon himself put not forth thine hand." Then Satan went away from the Lord's presence.

Not long after this things began to change with Job. Four messengers came to tell Job their sad news. The first messenger told Job that some enemies had stolen his oxen and donkeys. The second one told Job that his sheep had been destroyed by fire from heaven. The third one told him the Chaldeans had taken his camels. The fourth messenger told Job that all his children had been killed by a terrible windstorm while they were feasting in the oldest son's house.

In one day Job lost his children, his cattle, and his flocks. Suddenly he became poor. Then Job fell down upon the ground, and said, "The Lord gave, and the Lord hath taken away; blessed be the name of the Lord." So you see that Job had not lost everything. He had kept the most important thing in life, his faith in God.

Once again the angels appeared before the Lord. Satan, the trouble-maker, came also. The Lord said to him, "From whence comest thou?" Satan answered, "From going to and fro in the earth, and from walking up and down in it."

God asked Satan once more if he had noticed Job. Satan knew that all God said about Job was true. Job had remained true to God in spite of all his trouble, but Satan said to the Lord, "All that he hath will a man give for his life. But put forth thy hand now, and touch his bone and his flesh, and he will curse thee to thy face." The Lord said to Satan, "Behold, he is in thine hand; but save his life."

Satan went away. Not long after this Job was covered from his head to his feet with dreadful boils. He was in pain and misery day and night. Job's wife said to him one day, "Dost thou still retain thine integrity? Curse God, and die." Job answered, "Thou speakest as one of the foolish women speaketh. What? shall we receive good at the hand of God, and shall we not receive evil?" In all this Job did not sin with his lips.

When Job's three friends heard of his trouble they came to visit him. They did not bring him much comfort because they believed Job had done some very bad sin. They believed God was punishing Job. Although they made long speeches, Job did not know why these troubles came. Of one thing Job was sure. Job believed that God never did wrong.

At last God Himself spoke to Job and to his three friends. God was angry with Job's friends. God said to them, "…ye have not spoken of me the thing that is right, as my servant Job hath." The Lord commanded them to bring a burnt offering to Job. God wanted Job to pray for his friends.

After Job had prayed for his friends, God blessed him with many blessings. The Lord gave him twice as much as he had before. God gave Job seven sons again and also three daughters. In all the land there were no women so fair as the daughters of Job.

Job lived one hundred forty years after this and died being very old.

QUESTIONS ON LESSON 1

1. *What do we know about Job?*
   Job was a God-fearing man who lived in the land of Uz.
2. *What terrible thing happened when God gave Job's possessions into Satan's power?*
   In one day Job lost all his possessions and his children.
3. *What happened when God gave Job into Satan's hands?*
   Job was covered with dreadful boils from head to foot.
4. *What did Job's wife say to him when he was sick?*
   Job's wife said to him, "Curse God, and die."
5. *What did Job's friends do when they visited him?*
   Job's three friends made long speeches but did not comfort him.
6. *How did God bless Job for remaining faithful to Him?*
   God made Job well and gave him children again and great riches.

Exercise 1 (True or False)

1. Satan said Job served God because God blessed him. _____
   (Job 1:9, 10)
2. Job lost all his possessions in one day. _____ (Job 1:13-19)
3. When Job was sick nobody came to see him. _____ (Job 2:11)

Exercise 2 (Fill in Blanks)

1. Satan said to God, "Doth Job fear God for _____?"
   (Job 1:9)
2. Job's wife said to Job, "_____ God, and _____." (Job 2:9)
3. Job said, "For I know that my _____ liveth."
   (Job 19:25)
4. After Job's sickness, God gave Job _____ sons and _____
   daughters. (Job 42:13)

Something to Think About

1. Is Satan a person, or some evil desire?
2. Is sickness always the result of some awful sin we have done?
3. Was Job's sickness a punishment from God?

Memory Verse: Job 1:21b.
The Lord gave, and the Lord hath taken away;
blessed be the name of the Lord.

Lesson 2
JOSHUA LEADS THE ISRAELITES INTO CANAAN

Read: Joshua 1-4

After Moses died, the Israelites were still encamped on the east side of the Jordan River. Then the Lord said to Joshua, "Moses my servant is dead; now therefore arise, go over this Jordan, thou, and all this people, unto the land which I do give to them, even to the children of Israel" (Josh. 1:2).

God chose Joshua to be the second leader of Israel. God told him that He would be with him just as He had been with Moses. The Lord encouraged Joshua by telling him that all the land on which he walked would be given to the children of Israel. No man would be too strong for Joshua to conquer, if Joshua would remain obedient to God's Word.

Joshua obeyed God. He commanded his officers to tell the people to prepare food for the journey, for in three days they were to cross the Jordan River. This seemed like a very bold command. At that time of the year the Jordan River was much larger than at other times. And just across the Jordan were strong nations living in walled cities. There was the big city of Jericho with its high walls, which were so thick that houses were built on top of them. The large iron gates in the walls were closed every night to keep out the enemies. But this did not discourage Joshua. He trusted in the Lord his God!

Joshua sent out two spies to see what the land was like. He wanted to know what kind of people lived there.

The spies first went to the city of Jericho. There they stayed in the house of a woman named Rahab. This woman, as well as many other Canaanites, had heard fearful stories of the mighty God of the Israelites. The Canaanites were not so ready to give up their land and cities. But when they thought of Israel's God they became afraid and faint-hearted.

Rahab had been a heathen all her life. But now God placed in her heart the desire to take the great God of Israel for her own. She wanted to help God's people, and was friendly to the spies.

Certain Canaanites had seen the spies enter Rahab's home. They quickly told their king. He at once sent out soldiers to find them. When they came to Rahab's house she hid the spies on the flat roof of her house among some stalks of flax. When the soldiers asked Rahab about the spies, she said, "There came men unto me but I wist not whence they were." She told the soldiers that the men had gone out just about the time when the gates were closed when it was dark. She said that she did not know where they had gone. She said, "Pursue after them quickly; for ye shall overtake them." This was a lie; but Rahab was a heathen, and she believed in her heart she should help these Israelite men.

The soldiers quickly left to pursue the spies. Then Rahab told the spies, who were still safely hidden on the roof, that she believed that the Lord would give Israel all their land and cities. She told them all that she had heard about the doings of Israel's God. Rahab said, "The Lord your God, He is God in heaven above, and in the earth beneath."

Then Rahab and the spies made an agreement. The spies promised that Rahab and her family and their belongings would be saved when Jericho was destroyed. Rahab in turn promised to keep secret her conversation with the spies. Then she took a scarlet rope and let down the spies through an open window from her house on the wall. She left the scarlet rope in the window, so that the spies would know her house when they returned to destroy the city. After hiding in the mountains three days, the spies crossed the Jordan River and told Joshua all about their experience.

Then Joshua commanded the Israelites to get ready for the journey at once. Early in the morning the procession was formed. First came the priests carrying the chest called the Ark of the Covenant. Then followed all the Israelites marching in regular order.

The waters of the Jordan River were wild and turbulent. At Joshua's command the priests stepped into the water, and look, the waters stopped flowing down! The waters formed a high wall on two sides. There was a path for the Israelites to cross over. When the river bottom was dry the priests walked to the middle of the river. While they stood still, all the Israelites passed by them to the other side.

Joshua told twelve strong men each to pick up a large stone from the riverbed. These stones were put on a pile for a memorial for the future children of Israel.

When all the people had crossed over, the Jordan River flowed on as before. Now the Israelites were in the Promised Land.

QUESTIONS ON LESSON 2

1. *How long did the Israelites live in the desert?*
   The Israelites lived in the desert for forty years.
2. *How did Joshua find out about the land and people of Canaan?*
   Joshua sent two men to spy out the city of Jericho.
3. *Who was Rahab?*
   Rahab was a woman of Jericho who protected the spies.
4. *How did the spies get out of the city?*
   Rahab let the spies down out of a window by a scarlet rope.
5. *How did the Israelites cross the Jordan River?*
   God made: the riverbed dry before them.
6. *How did Joshua help the Israelites to remember God's great work?*
   Joshua raised up a heap of twelve large stones for a memorial.

Exercise 1 (True or False)

1. After Moses' death, Saul became the leader of Israel. _____
   (Josh. 1:1-9)
2. Joshua sent twelve spies to the city of Jericho. _____
3. Rahab was an Israelite woman who lived in Jericho. _____
4. God made a path through the Jordan River for Israel. _____
   (Josh. 3:7 -17)

Exercise 2 (Fill in Blanks)

1. _____ promised to help Joshua if he would obey Him.
2. The spies were kept hidden by _____. (Josh 2:1-7)
3. By _____ power the waters of the Jordan were held back.

Something to Think About

1. Are unchristian people always as fearless of God as they say?
2. Was salvation only for the Israelites in the Old Testament?
   See Joshua 6:25; Ruth 1:16, 17.

Memory Verse: Psalm 28:7.
The Lord is my strength and my shield.

Lesson 3

ISRAEL'S VICTORY AT JERICHO
AND DEFEAT AT AI

Read: Joshua 6 and 7

After the Israelites had crossed the Jordan River they set up a new camp. The tents of the different tribes of Israel were set up in their order with the tabernacle in the middle. The camp was not very far from the city of Jericho.

The gates of Jericho were kept locked day and night. The people were afraid of the Israelites. They did not dare to go in or out. Their barns, filled with corn and grain, were outside the city. The Israelites helped themselves to this grain. They needed this food, for with the beginning of the harvest God had stopped giving His people manna from heaven.

The Lord said to Joshua, "See, I have given into thine hand Jericho, and the king thereof, and the mighty men of valour. And ye shall compass the city, all ye men of war, and go round about the city once. Thus shalt thou do six days. And seven priests shall bear before the ark seven trumpets of rams' horns: and the seventh day ye shall compass the city seven times, and the priests shall blow with the trumpets. And it shall come to pass, that when they make a long blast with the ram's horn, and when ye hear the sound of the trumpet, all the people shall shout with a great shout; and the wall of the city shall fall down flat, and the people shall ascend up every man straight before him." This must have sounded strange to Joshua, but he trusted in the Lord.

Joshua did as the Lord commanded. For six days the Israelites went round about the city once each day. On the seventh day they started out early and went around the city six times. Once more they circled the city. When the priests blew their trumpets Joshua cried, "Shout, for the Lord hath given you the city." The soldiers shouted and down came the walls of the city with a great crash! But God spared that part of the wall on which Rahab's house stood and it remained standing.

The soldiers went into the city and killed every man, woman and child. They also killed all their animals. God had commanded them to destroy everything. Only Rahab and her family were saved, as the spies

11

had promised. After this Rahab went to live among the Israelites. She now worshipped the true God.

The Lord had commanded that all the silver and gold, brass and iron were to be put into the Lord's treasury. But a man named Achan saw a beautiful coat, a wedge of gold and some silver. He took these things home and hid them in the earthen floor of his tent. He thought that no one saw it, or knew of it.

Not far from Jericho was a small town called Ai. Joshua sent some men to find out about this city. They returned saying, "Let not all the people go up; but let about two or three thousand men go up and smite Ai... for they are but few." After the glorious victory at Jericho the Israelites thought they could easily conquer this small city. But the men of Ai beat the Israelites and killed thirty-six of them.

How discouraged the Israelites were after this defeat! Joshua was so discouraged that he tore his clothes, and put dust on his head. The elders of Israel did the same. They fell on their faces before the ark of the Lord. Joshua cried to the Lord and told Him how discouraged he was.

The Lord told Joshua to get up because there was a good reason why Israel had been beaten: they had sinned in that someone had taken things that belonged to the Lord. That was the reason why God had not blessed them with victory. Remember, Achan was the thief!

Upon God's command, Joshua rose up early and brought all the tribes of Israel together. God made known to Joshua that one man of the tribe of Judah had sinned. That man was Achan.

Joshua told Achan that he should confess to the Lord all that he had done. Then Achan confessed that when he saw the beautiful coat, the gold and the silver, he had coveted them and taken them. He also told Joshua where they were.

Joshua said to Achan, "Why hast thou troubled us? the Lord shall trouble thee this day." Then all Israel took Achan and his family and stoned them to death. His oxen and sheep and all his possessions were also destroyed. That was Achan's punishment for stealing the things that belonged to God. Now Israel was again free from God's anger.

QUESTIONS ON LESSON 3

1. *What strange orders did God give Joshua?*
   The Israelites were told to march around Jericho once a day for six days, and seven times on the seventh day.
2. *What happened when the Israelites obeyed God's command?*
   The walls of Jericho fell down.
3. *Which inhabitants of Jericho were saved alive?*
   Only Rahab and her family were spared.
4. *What did God command Joshua to do with the spoil of Jericho?*
   God commanded Joshua to put all the precious things into the Lord's treasury.
5. *How did Achan show his disobedience?*
   Achan stole some gold and silver, and a beautiful coat.
6. *What was the result of Achan's disobedience?*
   The Israelites could not conquer the city of Ai.

Exercise 1 (True or False)

1. Joshua and the Israelites attacked Jericho with swords and spears. _____
2. On the seventh day the walls of Jericho fell down. _____
3. Every last one of Jericho's people was killed by Israel. _____ (Josh. 6:21)
4. Achan was a thief and was never found out. _____ (Josh. 7:19, 20)

Exercise 2 (Fill in Blanks)

1. God told Joshua how to conquer the city of _____.
2. Only _____ was spared of all the people of Jericho.
3. Achan stole things that belonged to the _____.

Something to Think About

1. How can you prove that Achan knew that he was stealing?
2. Who said, "Be sure your sins will find you out"? (Num. 32:23)
3. Did the value of what Achan stole determine God's punishment for Achan or were there other reasons?

Memory Verse: Numbers 32:23.
Be sure your sins will find you out.

13

Lesson 4
THANKSGIVING AFTER VICTORY
Read: Joshua 8

Now that Israel was again right with God, the Lord encouraged Joshua, saying, "Fear not, neither be thou dismayed: take all the people of war with thee and arise, go up to Ai: see, I have given into thy hand the king of Ai, and his people, and his city, and his land." This was good news to Joshua. Shortly before this he had been bitterly disappointed. Now the Lord said that He would help the Israelites to conquer the city. God also told them that they might have for themselves whatever they should find in the city of Ai. But they had to kill the king and his people.

The Lord told Joshua exactly how to attack this city. We may believe that Joshua was more careful than ever to obey God's command. Joshua chose thirty thousand brave soldiers, and secretly sent them to Ai at night. These were to go to the other side of the city and hide themselves. Another five thousand were hid on the west side of the city.

Early in the morning Joshua took all the rest of the soldiers with him. He marched right up to the city as if to attack it. The king of Ai saw Joshua's army coming. He immediately prepared to fight them. As soon as the soldiers of Ai came out to fight the Israelites, Joshua and his men fled from the city, pretending to be afraid. This was done to draw the king of Ai and his soldiers out of his city.

The king of Ai did just as Joshua had expected. Every last soldier left the city and followed quickly after Joshua and his men. As soon as the army was quite a distance from the city the Lord said to Joshua, "Stretch out the spear that is in thine hand toward Ai, for I will give it into thy hand." And Joshua stretched out his spear toward the city. The men in hiding rushed into the city, which the king of Ai had left unprotected. There was not a man left to guard it.

The Israelite soldiers set fire to the city. When the king of Ai and his army looked back, they saw the smoke of their burning city. Then their courage left them.

When Joshua saw the smoke he knew that his soldiers were in the city. He and his soldiers turned upon the soldiers of Ai. They were soon beaten by Joshua and his army. The Israelites surrounded them on every side and killed them all as God had commanded. Also in the city all the women and children were killed. Joshua did not stop until every last one was destroyed.

This was God's judgment upon the wicked people of Ai. These people, like the people of Jericho and other cities of Canaan, were idol worshippers. God was angry with them for all their wickedness.

After Ai was conquered Joshua led the Israelites on over the mountains, until they came to the city of Shechem. The people of Canaan had heard about Jericho and Ai. They were filled with fear and did not dare to resist the Israelites. Near Shechem were two mountains, Ebal on the north and Gerizim on the south, with a valley between. There, Joshua gathered all the people of Israel, together with their wives and children.

In the middle of this valley Joshua built an altar of uncut stone. On this new altar the Israelites offered to the Lord, and they worshipped Him. Joshua wrote on these uncut stones a copy of the law of Moses. He did this in the presence of the people of Israel.'

Joshua knew that the Israelites could not overcome their enemies without God's blessing. He felt that it was necessary to instruct the people in God's Word and to take time for worship. So Joshua read the law, which Moses had written. He also read God's words of blessing. All the people, including the women and children, listened carefully to the reading of the law. Half of the tribes stood on the slope of Mt. Ebal on the north. The other half of the tribes stood on the slope of Mt. Gerizim on the south. What a beautiful sight that must have been!

After the Israelites had worshipped the Lord, they marched down the mountains, past the smoldering ruins of Ai. They also came past the heap of stones where Achan was buried, and past the broken walls of Jericho. These all reminded them of God's blessing upon Israel and God's punishment upon the wicked. Finally, they came back to their camp at Gilgal beside the Jordan River.

QUESTIONS ON LESSON 4

1. *How did God help Israel after Achan had been stoned?*
   God helped Israel to capture the city of Ai.
2. *What did Joshua do with the people of Ai?*
   Joshua killed the king of Ai and all his people, as God had commanded.
3. *What did God tell Israel to do with the spoils of Ai?*
   God told the Israelites that they might keep the spoils of Ai for themselves.
4. *What did the Israelites do after Ai had been conquered?*
   The Israelites offered sacrifices of thanksgiving and worshipped God.
5. *What did Joshua read in the presence of the Israelites?*
   Joshua read the Word of God that the Lord had given to Moses.
6. *Why did Joshua take time to offer sacrifices and to worship God?*
   Joshua wanted to teach the Israelites that they depended upon God for help in battle.

Exercise 1 (True or False)

1. After Achan's death, God promised Joshua victory over the king of Ai. _____
2. If God promises blessings we can be careless. _____ (Josh. 1:8)
3. Israel's enemies were strong but God was stronger. _____
4. After the victory Joshua taught the people how to be thankful. _____ (Josh. 8:30-35)

Exercise 2 (Fill in Blanks)

1. God said to Joshua, " Be _____ and of good _____." (Josh. 1:9)
2. The king of _____ left his city unprotected.
3. Israel took all the _____ and the spoil for themselves from Ai. (Josh. 8:27)
4. Joshua took the Israelites to the mountains to offer sacrifices of _____ to God.

Something to Think About

1. When the Israelites obeyed God, then God blessed them with victory.
2. Since God had promised Joshua the victory, was it necessary for Joshua to be careful?
3. Of what song are you reminded as you read the last part of our story?

Memory Verse: Psalm 66:18.
If I regard iniquity in my heart, the Lord will not hear me.

Lesson 5

ISRAEL DECEIVED BUT AGAIN VICTORIOUS

Read: Joshua 9 and 10

The news of all that Joshua and the Israelites had done at Jericho and Ai soon spread through the land. The people were filled with fear when they heard how Israel's God was making Joshua and his soldiers strong.

Not far from Ai lived the Gibeonites. They too were fearful of the Israelites. They saw that Israel's God was helping them to conquer every city. They knew also that Joshua and his men could come upon them any day.

As they were talking about this, someone suggested a plan to trick the Israelites. The Gibeonites put on old and ragged clothes. They wore dirty worn-out shoes. They took with them bread that was dry and mouldy. In that way they came to Joshua at Gilgal. They acted as if they were strangers who had come from a far country.

When the Gibeonites met Joshua, they said, "We be come from a far country: now therefore make ye a league with us." The Israelites said to them, "Peradventure ye dwell among us; and how shall we make a league with you?"

The Gibeonites told Joshua that they had come because they had heard what God had done for Israel in Egypt. They knew that God had helped Israel to conquer the two kings of the Amorites. They said, "Our elders spake to us saying, Take food with you for the journey, and go to meet them, and say unto them, We are your servants; therefore make ye a league with us."

They told Joshua that the bread that they had taken hot from their ovens when they left was now dry and mouldy. The bottles for their wine, which had been new when they started on their journey, were now old and torn. Their garments and shoes had become old and worn because of their long journey.

The Gibeonites made everything look so real that Joshua and the princes of Israel believed them. Instead of first asking the Lord what they should do, Joshua and the princes made an agreement with the Gibeonites. They swore an oath that they would let them live.

After three days the Israelites heard that the Gibeonites were close neighbours. They were not strangers at all! This made the Israelites very angry. They were ready to make war against them. But the princes said, "We will even let them live, lest wrath be upon us, because of the oath which we sware unto them…. But let them be hewers of wood and drawers of water unto all the congregation." So the Gibeonites were saved alive as the princes had promised them. The Gibeonites did not like their work, but it was better than to be destroyed by war.

When the kings of the other cities heard how that the Gibeonites had made peace with Israel, they became angry and prepared to fight against them. Five kings grouped their armies together to destroy the Gibeonites. When the Gibeonites heard that the kings were going to fight them, they went to Joshua. They asked him to help them. The Lord said to Joshua, "Fear them not: for I have delivered them into thine hand."

Joshua and his army came upon the enemy suddenly and put them to flight. As Israel pursued the enemy, the Lord helped Joshua by sending a terrible hailstorm. More Canaanites were killed by the large hailstones than by Joshua's soldiers. Joshua was very eager for a complete victory over the enemy. He prayed to the Lord and said in the presence of Israel, "Sun, stand thou still upon Gibeon, and thou, Moon, in the valley of Aijalon." God heard Joshua's prayer. For the only time in history the sun and the moon stood still for about a day.

The five kings fled into a cave. Joshua's soldiers kept them there safely by rolling big stones upon the mouth of the cave. When the Israelites returned from pursuing the enemy, Joshua told the soldiers to open the mouth of the cave and bring out the five kings. He hanged the five kings on five trees. When Israel returned to Gilgal, they had conquered all the south country, and had destroyed all the people.

After this, all the kings of the north came together to fight Israel. Thousands upon thousands of soldiers, with chariots and horses, came to war with Israel. But God told Joshua not to fear.

Battle after battle was fought until finally Hazor, the capitol city, was also destroyed. It took Israel a long time, but when all the cities were conquered Joshua had subdued thirty-one kings. These and their people were killed because of their wickedness against the Lord. God gave the land to Israel so that they might worship Him in this good land.

QUESTIONS ON LESSON 5

1. *What effect did Joshua's victory over Ai have upon the neighbouring cities?*
   The heathen kings were afraid of the Israelites and Israel's God.
2. *How did the Gibeonites deceive Joshua into making an agreement with them?*
   The Gibeonites acted as if they were friendly strangers from a far country.
3. *What mistake did Joshua make?*
   Joshua did not ask the Lord what he should do about the Gibeonites.
4. *What did Joshua do to the Gibeonites for deceiving him?*
   Joshua made the Gibeonites servants to cut wood and draw water.
5. *How did God help Israel conquer the five kings of the south?*
   The Lord rained great hailstones upon Israel's enemy.
6. *What miracle took place as a result of Joshua's prayer?*
   God caused the sun and moon to stand still until the enemy was destroyed.

Exercise 1 (True or False)

1. Israel's God was their strong defense and power. _____
2. The Gibeonites tricked Joshua into making a treaty with them._____
3. Joshua did not ask the Lord what he should do with the Gibeonites. _____
4. The Gibeonites were glad to become Israel's servants. _____

Exercise 2 (Fill in Blanks)

1. The Gibeonites acted as if they came from a far _____.
2. Joshua did not dare to destroy the Gibeonites because of the _____.
3. Joshua prayed "_____, stand thou still upon Gibeon, and thou _____ in the valley of Aijalon." (Josh. 10:12)
4. Joshua conquered _____ kings in the land of Canaan. (Josh. 12:24)

Something to Think About

1. Can you give any reason why Joshua did not ask God about the Gibeonites first?
2. What good advice does God give us in Proverbs 3:6?
3. God helped His people Israel in many ways. Think of the hailstones and of the sun and moon standing still. Does this have any meaning for Christians today?

Memory Verse: Proverbs 3:6.
In all thy ways acknowledge him, and he shall direct thy paths.

Lesson 6

EACH TRIBE RECEIVES A SHARE OF THE LAND

Read: Joshua 13-24

Finally the entire land of Canaan had been conquered. The time had come for Joshua to divide the land. The Lord directed Joshua in making the choice for each tribe. Each tribe received a share according to its size. The larger tribes like Judah, Simeon and Manasseh received large shares. The smaller tribes of Dan and Benjamin received smaller ones.

The people of Israel had been counted when they first came out of Egypt. Just before the Israelites entered the land of Canaan a second census was taken. All the men of twenty years and older were counted.

There were twelve tribes. The tribe of Levi was to be kept separate because they were set aside for service in the tabernacle. In the eleven tribes there were over six hundred thousand men who were able to fight. The tribe of Levi numbered twenty-three thousand men. In all, counting men, women and children, the number of Israelites was about three million.

In this second census there were only two men whose names were numbered in the first census. These were Joshua and Caleb. All the other men who at that time were twenty years and older could not enter the land of Canaan. They had not believed God's Word. As punishment they had all died during the forty years in the wilderness. Their children had now taken their places.

The tribes of Reuben, Gad and the half tribe of Manasseh had asked for the territory on the east side of the Jordan River. These tribes had large flocks of cows and sheep. The rich and fertile fields of Moab were just the place for these tribes. Moses had given them permission to leave their wives and children there, providing the men would go along to help the other tribes conquer Canaan.

Now that Canaan had been conquered, Joshua gathered the men of these tribes together. He told them that they had done all that Moses, God's servant, commanded them. They had faithfully helped the other tribes. Now they could go back to their homes where their wives and children were waiting for them. Joshua warned them never to forget to worship God and to obey Him with all their heart.

The tribe of Levi received forty-eight cities. The people of this tribe were to live in cities and not to have large farms. Around each city there was enough land for their cows and sheep, but no more.

Six of these cities were chosen to be "cities of refuge." If anyone should happen to kill some person by accident, he might run into one of these cities. Here he would be safe from punishment. Three cities of refuge were located on each side of the Jordan River.

All the other tribes received their shares as the Lord directed Joshua. The Israelites had everything that their heart could desire. All the cattle and sheep, the gold, brass, iron and precious things that the Canaanites possessed, now belonged to God's chosen people. The houses and orchards, which the heathen people enjoyed, were now the property of the Israelites.

You probably wonder whether the Israelites did right in taking all these things away from the heathens. They surely did, for God had commanded them to do so. The heathen people did not use the things God had given them in the right way. God has a right to give them to whomsoever He desires.

A beautiful spot was chosen for the tabernacle. It was set up in Shiloh. The place was just about in the middle of the country. This made it easy for all the tribes to come to worship God in His house.

Three times each year the Israelites came together for special feast days. These were the Passover feast, when the lamb was killed and roasted and eaten with unleavened bread; the feast of Tabernacles, when the Israelites made huts of branches and twigs and they lived outdoors for a week; and the feast of Pentecost, fifty days after the Passover, when the first ripe harvest was brought to God's altar. All three feasts were held at Shiloh.

At Caleb's request, Joshua gave him the city of Hebron. You will remember that he was one of the faithful spies Moses sent out to Canaan. With God's help Caleb conquered the heathen giants of Hebron. His family became the owners of that land.

Joshua lived to be one hundred and ten years old. Before he died, Joshua warned the people not to become friendly with the heathen people. He wanted the Israelites to worship the only true and living God.

QUESTIONS ON LESSON 6

1. *How was the land of Canaan divided among the Israelites?*
   God directed Joshua to give each tribe a part of the land according to its size.
2. *What share did the tribe of Levi receive?*
   The Levites received forty-eight cities and their suburbs.
3. *Where did the Israelites set up the tabernacle?*
   The tabernacle was set up in Shiloh.
4. *Which three feasts did Israel keep each year?*
   The Israelites kept the Passover feast, the feast of Tabernacles, and the feast of Pentecost.
5. *To whom did Joshua give the city of Hebron?*
   Joshua gave Hebron to Caleb, one of the faithful spies.
6. *What parting message did Joshua give to Israel before he died?*
   Joshua commanded Israel to serve the Lord sincerely and truly.

Exercise 1 (True or False)

1. Joshua divided the land as he thought best. ____ (Josh. 14:5)
2. Joshua chose eight cities of refuge for Israel. _____
3. Caleb and Joshua received their reward for faithful service. _____
4. The tabernacle was set up in Hebron. _____

Exercise 2 (Fill in Blanks)

1. The tribe of Levi received _____ - _____ cities.
2. _____ cities of refuge were chosen by Joshua.
3. God gave Israel _____ feasts to keep every year.
4. _____ reminded Joshua of _____ promise forty-five years before.

Something to Think About

1. A special place was chosen for the tabernacle (tent-church) of Israel.
2. Israel had great feasts every year. What church holidays do we have?

Memory Verse: Psalm 37:3.
Trust in the Lord and do good; so shalt thou dwell in the land.

Lesson 7

THE ISRAELITES RULED BY JUDGES

Read: Judges 2 and 3

How wonderfully God cared for His people Israel! All the way from Egypt to Canaan God protected them. When they came into Canaan God helped them drive out the Canaanites. God gave the possessions of the heathen peoples to the Israelites. One would think that the people of Israel would never forget God or forsake Him.

But after Joshua died another generation of people grew up. The first generation had made a very serious mistake. They had not destroyed all the heathen peoples as God had commanded. After a while, some of the heathen people lived right among the Israelites. They even married some of them.

To the east were the Moabites, to the west were the Philistines, and to the south were the Edomites. All these bowed down to images. Some of them even offered and burned their own children upon the idol altars.

Some well-known idols these heathen people served were Baal and Ashtaroth of the Canaanites, Molech of the Moabites, and Dagon of the Philistines. Those who worshipped these idols also lived in sin.

As time went on the people of Israel also began to neglect the worship of the only true and living God. They began to live somewhat like the heathens. It was not long before they worshipped idols along with the heathen people.

The Lord God looked down from heaven and He saw the evil deeds of Israel. So God gave them into the hands of their enemies. Their enemies came upon them and took away their grain, their grapes, and their olive oil. This made the people very poor.

The first heathen king who tried to rob the Israelites was the king of Mesopotamia. He led his army into the land and made Israel serve him for eight years. In their anguish the people prayed to God. The Lord answered them by sending them a man named Othniel. He was the younger brother of Caleb, one of the faithful spies. Othniel set the Israelites free from their enemy and ruled Israel. For forty years the land had rest, and then Othniel died.

Again the Israelites forgot God and worshipped idols. Because of this sin God caused another enemy to rise up against them. This time it was the Moabites who made war against Israel and conquered them. The name of the king of Moab was Eglon. Eglon ruled Israel for eighteen years.

The Israelites did not like Eglon to reign over them. In their trouble the Israelites remembered God and prayed to Him for help. God heard their cry and He raised up another deliverer. This time it was Ehud, the second judge of Israel. He was a man of the tribe of Benjamin.

One day the Israelites sent Ehud to Moab. Ehud carried with him a present for the king. But underneath his cloak, fastened on his right side, he also carried a sharp, two-edged dagger about a foot and a half long.

When Ehud arrived in Moab, he went to the palace. He asked to see the king. He found the king sitting in his room. After he had presented the gift to king Eglon, he said, "I have a secret message for you, O King." The king sent all the other people from the room. Then Ehud said again, "I have a message to you from God." As King Eglon rose from his chair, Ehud put his left hand underneath his cloak and pulled out the dagger he had hidden there. He thrust it into the body of the king, and the king fell to the floor.

When Ehud saw that the king was dead, he locked the doors of the room. Then he escaped by way of the porch. Quickly he fled to his own country.

The servants of Eglon waited a long time for Ehud to come out of the room. At last they tried the doors of the room. They found them locked. They thought the king must be sleeping and that he had locked the doors so that he would not be disturbed. After a long time, the servants began to realize that something was wrong. They took a key and opened the door. There they found their king upon the floor.

In the meantime Ehud had called the army of Israel together to fight against Moab. Since Moab's king was dead, they had no leader. The Israelites gained the victory easily. Ten thousand Moabites were killed in the battle. This was the end of Israel's warfare with the Moabites. Never again did they trouble the Israelites. God now gave His people rest for eighty years.

QUESTIONS ON LESSON 7

1   *How did Israel disobey God's command as to the heathen people of Canaan?*
   The Israelites did not destroy all the Canaanites.
2. *What did the heathen people do to the Israelites?*
   The heathen people caused the Israelites to forget God, and to worship idols.
3. *How did God punish the Israelites for their sin?*
   God gave the Israelites into the hands of their enemies.
4. *What did the Israelites do when God punished them?*
   The people were sorry for their sins and prayed God to help them.
5. *How did the Lord answer the prayers of the Israelites?*
   God raised up judges to set Israel free.
6. *What did Othniel, the first judge, do?*
   Othniel delivered Israel from the Mesopotamians.
7. *What did Ehud do as a judge?*
   Ehud freed the Israelites from the Moabites by killing their king.

Exercise 1 (True or False)

1. God never gave Israel any law about worshipping idols. _____ (Ex. 20:3)
2. God told the Israelites to marry heathen people. _____ (Deut. 7:3)
3. When Israel cried to God He helped them. _____

Exercise 2 (Fill in Blanks)

1. When Israel became friendly with the heathens they _____ to God. (Judg. 2:12)
2. When Israel prayed to God then God sent them _____. (Judg. 2:16)
3. Othniel, the first judge, was _____ younger brother. (Judg. 3:9)

Something to Think About

1. Why was it wrong for the Israelites to be friendly with the Canaanites?
2. What danger do you see in having all kinds of non-Christian friends?
3. Were it not for God's mercy and power Israel would have perished.

Memory Verse: Psalm 30:2.
O Lord my God, I cried unto thee, and thou hast healed me.

25

Lesson 8

THE ISRAELITES RULED BY JUDGES

Read: Judges 4 and 5

How sad that after God delivered Israel out of the hands of the enemies, they again forgot God and worshipped idols. The people became
so wicked that we read, "Every man did that which was right in his
own eyes."

God sent another enemy to punish the Israelites. This time it was
Jabin, king of the Canaanites. King Jabin had a large and strong army.
He had 900 chariots of iron that he used in battle. The Israelites had no
chariots, and very few weapons of war. The Canaanites took away the
shields and spears of the Israelites. It was not safe for the people of Israel
to be on the highways. Women were harmed and killed at the wells
when they went to draw water. For twenty years king Jabin oppressed
the northern tribes of Israel.

Once more Israel remembered God and cried to Him. At that time
Israel was ruled by a woman named Deborah. She was the fourth judge
of Israel. Deborah was a wise and a God-fearing woman, and trusted in
God. Deborah lived in a tent under a palm tree. Whenever the people of Israel needed help or advice they would come to Deborah. God
spoke to the people through Deborah, and she obeyed God in all His
commandments.

One day Deborah sent for a soldier of Israel named Barak. Deborah
told him that God wanted him to take ten thousand soldiers to fight
against Sisera, the captain of Jabin's army. She told Barak that God
would give him the victory.

But Barak was fearful. He did not trust in God, as he should. Barak
said to Deborah, "If thou wilt go with me, I will go: but if thou wilt not
go with me, then I will not go."

Deborah was not afraid. She believed that God's power was all that
was necessary to deliver Israel from the enemy. Deborah told Barak
she would go with him, but God would give the honour of victory to a
woman.

Barak gathered his ten thousand soldiers together and went up to
Mount Tabor. Deborah was with them. Sisera heard that Barak was coming. He gathered his 900 chariots of iron and his army, and encamped in
the valley below Mount Tabor by the side of the River Kishon.

At the command of Deborah, Barak and his soldiers swooped down from Mount Tabor upon Sisera and his warriors. Then God sent a fearful storm, which made the Kishon River to over-flow its banks. The chariots stuck fast in the wet ground. Many of Sisera's army were swept away by the flood and drowned. The Israelites killed many of Sisera's soldiers with the sword. Although the army of Sisera was much larger than Israel's army, Israel was victorious. God was fighting for Israel.

Sisera escaped on foot. He ran until he was very tired. At last he came to the tent of a woman named Jael. Jael was neither an Israelite nor a Canaanite. She was a Kenite. Sisera thought that Jael was a friend. He did not know that she favoured Israel. Jael pretended to be friendly with Sisera.

She went out to meet Sisera and said, "Turn in, my lord, turn in to me; fear not." He asked for a drink of water, and she gave him some milk. He laid down to rest, and she covered him with a blanket. Sisera was soon sound asleep. Then Jael took a long tent pin, like a very long nail, and hammered it right through Sisera's head and into the ground.

Later, as Jael stood in the door of her tent, Barak came by, looking for Sisera. Jael called to him and said, "Come, and I will show you the man whom thou seekest."

When Barak entered the tent, he found Sisera dead. Jael had killed the general of the Canaanite army. The honour of victory went to a woman, as God had said.

Deborah and Barak sang for gladness, praising God for His deliverance and victory. God now gave His people rest for forty years.

QUESTIONS ON LESSON 8

1. *How does the Bible describe the sin of Israel in the time of the judges?*
   "Every man did that which was right in his own eyes."
2. *What do we know about Deborah, the fourth judge of Israel?*
   Deborah was a wise woman who trusted in God.
3. *What did Deborah do at God's command?*
   Deborah called Barak to lead Israel's army.
4. *Was Barak ready to go to war with the Canaanites?*
   Barak would not go to the battle unless Deborah went with him.
5. *How did Israel overcome the army of the Canaanites?*
   God helped Israel by sending a fearful storm.
6. *How was the captain of the Canaanite army killed?*
   Sisera was killed by a woman named Jael, while he lay sleeping in her tent.

Exercise 1 (True or False)

1. The king of Canaan had four hundred chariots of iron. _____ (Judg. 4:3)
2. Deborah sent Barak to battle at God's command. _____ (Judg. 4:6)
3. God gave Deborah and Barak courage for the battle. _____ (Judg. 4:7)
4. Israel won the victory because they had a strong army. _____ (Judg. 4:15)

Exercise 2 (Fill in Blanks)

1. When Israel sinned again, God sent king _____ to oppress them. (Judg. 4:1, 2)
2. When Israel cried to the Lord, God sent a woman judge named _____.
3. Jael went out to meet _____, and said to him, "_____ in, my lord." (Judg. 4:18)
4. Jael killed Sisera with a _____ and a nail. (Judg. 4:21)

Something to Think About

1. Why is it an advantage to a country to have God-fearing rulers?
2. Faith in God makes us strong.
3. What powers did God call into use to overcome the Canaanites? (Judg. 5)

Memory Verse: Isaiah 12:2a.
Behold, God is my salvation; I will trust, and not be afraid.

Lesson 9

THE ISRAELITES RULED BY JUDGES – *GIDEON*

Read: Judges 6, 7, 8

For forty years the children of Israel seemed to do well. But again they forgot the Lord and did evil. This time the Lord sent the Midianites to rob and capture them. The Israelites hid themselves in caves and dens in the mountains. In their fear they cried to the Lord for help. God sent a prophet to tell them of their sins.

After the prophet had done his work, God sent a man named Gideon to help Israel. One day, an angel of the Lord appeared to Gideon and said, "The Lord is with thee thou mighty man of valour." The angel said, "Go in this thy might, and thou shalt save Israel from the hand of the Midianites: have not I sent thee?"

Gideon answered the Lord, "Oh my Lord, wherewith shall I save Israel? behold, my family is poor in Manasseh, and I am the least in my father's house." The Lord said to Gideon, "Surely I will be with thee, and thou shalt smite the Midianites as one man." Then Gideon asked the angel for a sign so that he would know that this was from the Lord. Gideon brought out some meat and bread and broth. Then the angel of God said to Gideon, "Take the meat and the unleavened cakes and lay them upon this rock, and pour out the broth." Gideon did as the angel told him.

When the angel of the Lord touched the meat and the bread with the end of his staff, fire came out of the rock. It burned up the meat and the bread. After this the angel went away.

After this God told Gideon to break down the altar of Baal his father had built. One night Gideon and ten other men broke it down. Gideon built an altar unto the Lord and offered his father's bullock upon the altar.

Gideon asked the Lord once more to show him a sign. He said to the Lord, "If thou wilt save Israel by my hand as thou hast said, Behold, I will put a fleece of wool on the floor; and if the dew be on the fleece only, and it be dry upon all the earth besides, then shall I know that thou wilt save Israel by mine hand, as thou hast said."

In the morning Gideon looked at the fleece. It was wet with dew. He could wring a bowlful of water out of it. Then Gideon asked the Lord for one more sign. He asked the Lord to let the dew fall upon the earth and keep the fleece of wool dry. The Lord did that also for Gideon.

Then Gideon prepared a large army to fight the Midianites. God knew that if He saved Israel with so many soldiers Israel would give the honour of victory to themselves and not to God. So the Lord told Gideon to ask all those who were fearful and afraid to go home. About twenty-two thousand men went home. There were still ten thousand soldiers left.

The Lord said to Gideon, "The people are yet too many." God told Gideon to take his army to the water to drink. God said, "Everyone that lappeth of the water with his tongue, as a dog lappeth, him shalt thou set by himself; likewise everyone that boweth down upon his knees to drink." There were three hundred men who lapped the water with their tongue as a dog laps water. God told Gideon He would save Israel by using the three hundred men. The rest who bowed down upon their knees to drink, were sent home.

God encouraged Gideon by sending him close to the camp of the Midianites that night. There Gideon and his servant overheard a soldier telling about his dream. Then Gideon worshipped the Lord and prepared for the battle. He divided the three hundred men into three groups. He gave each man a trumpet and a pitcher with a lamp in it. He told the men to watch him. He said, "When I blow the trumpet, then blow ye the trumpets also on every side of the camp, and say, "The sword of the Lord, and of Gideon."

The three hundred men went to the camp of the Midianites. When Gideon blew his trumpet, they blew their trumpets. They broke the pitchers in which the lamps were hidden, and they cried, "The sword of the Lord, and of Gideon."

The Midianites were surprised and frightened at the loud noise and the lights. They ran in every direction. In their mad rush they fought and killed one another. They fled from Israel. But Gideon captured the two kings and their soldiers, and killed them.

Then the men of Israel wanted Gideon to be their king and his sons after him. Gideon told them that he would not rule over them, neither his sons. He said, "The Lord shall rule over you."

QUESTIONS ON LESSON 9

1. *Why did God deliver Israel into the hands of the Midianites?*
   The children of Israel again did evil in the sight of the Lord.
2. *How did God show His great love to the Israelites when they repented?*
   God sent a prophet to tell Israel about their sins.
3. *Whom did the Lord send after the prophet's work was done?*
   The Lord sent Gideon to become the fifth judge of Israel.
4. *What did Gideon ask of the Lord?*
   Gideon asked for a sign to prove that God had talked with him.
5. *How large was Gideon's army when he went to fight the Midianites?*
   The Lord allowed only three hundred men to go with Gideon.
6. *Why did the Lord allow Gideon only a small army?*
   God wanted to teach Israel that victory is of the Lord.

Exercise 1 (True or False)

1. When Israel sinned again, God sent the Midianites to oppress them.
   _____
2. God sent a prophet to call Gideon to become a judge. _____
   (Judg. 6:7-14)
3. Gideon was afraid to go in his own strength. _____ (Judg. 6: 25)
4. Gideon used thirty-two thousand men to fight the Midianites. _____
   (Judg. 7:1-8)

Exercise 2 (Fill in Blanks)

1. God said to Gideon, "Surely ___ will be with thee." (Judg. 6:16)
2. Gideon asked a sign of God with _____ of wool and the _____.
   (Judg. 6:37)
3. God said to Gideon, "By the three hundred men that _____
   will I save you." (Judg. 7:7)
4. The three hundred soldiers cried, "The sword of the _____ and of
   _____." (Judg. 7:20)

Something to Think About

1. How did God show His love for Israel?
2. Why did God choose the three hundred men who lapped water like
   a dog, to fight the Midianites?
3. Why did Gideon use such strange instruments like trumpets,
   pitchers and lamps for war?

Memory Verse: Judges 8:23b.
The Lord shall rule over you.

Lesson 10

SAMSON, THE STRONG MAN

Read: Judges 13:1 to 16:31

After Gideon died, the children of Israel again turned to idol worship. As at other times God allowed the heathen people to trouble Israel. This time it was the Philistines. The Israelites again cried to the Lord for help.

At that time there was a man of the tribe of Dan whose name was Manoah. One day an angel of the Lord promised Manoah's wife that she was to have a son. The angel told her that from his birth he was to be dedicated to the Lord. His hair must not be cut. He should never drink wine, nor eat anything unclean. The angel said, "He shall begin to deliver Israel out of the hands of the Philistines."

When the promised baby boy was born, his parents named him Samson. As the baby grew older, God made him very strong. When Samson became a full-grown man he went to a place called Timnath. There he fell in love with a Philistine woman. His parents did not like this but they agreed to go to visit the woman.

On their way to Timnath a lion roared at Samson. He took hold of the lion and tore him to pieces. When Samson returned home from Timnath he saw that a swarm of bees had made some honey in the dried-up body of the lion. Samson took some of the honey and ate it, and also gave some to his father and mother.

After this, Samson made a big wedding feast. There were thirty young men at the feast. Samson gave them a riddle. He told them if they could guess his riddle within seven days he would give them thirty shirts and thirty coats.

Samson told them his riddle. He said, "Out of the eater came forth meat, and out of the strong came forth sweetness." When the men could not guess the answer, they went to Samson's wife.

They said they would burn her and her father's house if she did not tell them. Samson's wife coaxed Samson to tell her the answer. After a while he gave her the answer. Quickly she told the young men. The young men came to Samson saying, "What is sweeter than honey? and what is stronger than a lion." Samson knew at once that his wife had told them.

32

Samson went out and killed thirty Philistines. He took their clothes and gave them to the young men to whom he had given the riddle. Then he went home angry, leaving his wife behind.

After some time Samson returned to visit his wife. He took a present for her. Her father told him she had been given to another man. Then Samson caught three hundred foxes, tied firebrands to their tails, and let them run into the fields of the Philistines. The fire burned the corn, the vineyards and the olive trees. When the Philistines heard that Samson had done this because Samson's wife had been given to another man, they burned her and her father with fire.

Then the Philistines went and camped against Judah. When the people of Judah asked them why they did this, they said, "To bind Samson are we come up, to do to him as he did to us." Three thousand men went to where Samson was staying. He agreed to be tied with two new ropes. When the Philistines shouted for joy because they had Samson captive, he broke the ropes and set himself free. Seeing the jawbone of a donkey, he took it and with it he killed one thousand Philistines.

One day Samson went to the city of Gaza. The Philistines heard of this and they locked the gates of the city to capture him. At night Samson rose up. He took the heavy gates, put them on his shoulders and carried them miles away to Hebron.

Some time later Samson fell in love with a woman named Delilah. The Philistines promised her much money if she could find out what made Samson so strong. After much sweet-talk Samson told her that he had been a Nazarite ever since his birth. If his hair were cut, he would lose his strength. One day when Samson was sleeping, Delilah asked a man to cut off his locks of hair. Then the Philistines came upon him and Samson had lost his strength. They took him, put out his eyes and put him in prison.

One day, the Philistines were in their temple making a sacrifice to Dagon, their god. They sent for Samson to entertain them. His hair was now grown again. He asked a boy to lead him to the pillars of the building. There were about three thousand Philistine men and women on the porch. Samson prayed and asked the Lord to make him strong. Samson put forth all his strength as he pulled at the pillars. The whole building came down with a crash. All the people were killed. Samson died with them. He had helped Israel by destroying many Philistines.

QUESTIONS ON LESSON 10

1. *What promise did God's angel give to Manoah's wife?*
   The angel promised Manoah's wife a son.
2. *What did Samson do on his way to Timnath?*
   Samson killed a lion.
3. *How did Samson once punish the Philistines?*
   Samson burned the crops of the Philistines with burning fox tails.
4. *What did Samson do at Gaza?*
   Samson took the gates of the city on his shoulders and carried them to Hebron.
5. *What did Delilah do when Samson was sleeping?*
   Delilah had Samson's long hair cut off while he slept.
6. *What did the Philistines do to Samson after he had lost his strength?*
   The Philistines put out Samson's eyes and put him in prison.
7. *How did Samson's life come to an end?*
   Samson died with thousands of Philistines when he pulled down a large temple.

Exercise 1 (True or False)

1. Manoah and his wife called their son Samuel._____
2. Samson married an Israelite woman. _____ (Judg. 14:1-7)
3. Samson killed a thousand Philistines with his sword. _____ (Judg. 15:15)
4. Samson killed more people at his death than when he was alive. _____ (Judg. 16:30)

Exercise 2 (Fill in Blanks)

1. God wanted Samson to be a _____. (Judg. 13:5)
2. Samson found _____ in the lion's body. (Judg. 14:8)
3. Samson killed one thousand Philistines with the _____ of a _____. (Judg. 15:15)
4. Delilah asked a man to cut off Samson's _____. (Judg. 16:19)

Something to Think About

1. Was Samson strong because he had long hair?
2. Was Samson wise in telling Delilah what made him so strong?

Memory Verse: Psalm 71:16.
I will go in the strength of the Lord God.

34

Lesson 11

RUTH MAKES A WISE CHOICE

Read: Ruth 1-4

At the time of the judges there was a man of Israel whose name was Elimelech. His wife's name was Naomi. They had two sons, Mahlon and Chilion. This family lived in the city of Bethlehem. They worshipped the true God.

Now there was a famine in the land of Canaan. Because of this Elimelech decided to move with his family across the Jordan River into Moab. There was no famine in Moab.

Naomi's husband died in Moab and she was left with her two sons. Both sons married women of Moab. The name of the one was Orpah and the name of the other was Ruth. After they had lived in Moab about ten years, Mahlon and Chilion also died. Now Naomi had lost her husband and her two sons.

One day she decided to return to Judah. Naomi had heard that the Lord had again blessed His people with food. It was a long walk to Bethlehem. Ruth and Orpah walked along with Naomi. After a while Naomi said to Ruth and Orpah, "Go, return each to your mother's house; the Lord deal kindly with you, as ye have dealt with the dead, and with me." After Naomi had asked the Lord to bless her daughters-in-law she kissed them and they all cried.

Orpah and Ruth said, "Surely we will return with thee unto thy people." When Naomi urged them to go back home they wept again. Finally Orpah kissed her mother-in-law goodbye and returned to Moab. But Ruth clung to Naomi. Then Naomi once more bade Ruth to go with Orpah, but she refused.

Ruth said to Naomi, "Entreat me not to leave thee, or to return from following thee: for whither thou goest, I will go; and where thou lodgest, I will lodge: thy people shall be my people, and thy God my God: Where thou diest, will I die, and there will I be buried: the Lord do so to me, and more also, if aught but death part thee and me." What wonderful words these are!

Naomi saw that Ruth had made a good choice. She took Ruth along to Bethlehem. The people of the city were surprised to see Naomi back. They came to meet her, and said, "Is this Naomi?" And she said, "Call me not Naomi (which means *sweetness*), call me Mara (which means *bitterness*): for the Lord hath dealt very bitterly with me."

Naomi and Ruth came to Bethlehem in the time of barley harvest. Naomi knew a rich man whose name was Boaz. He was related to her husband. Ruth asked Naomi if she might go to pick up grain that the reapers dropped as they harvested in the fields. Ruth happened to go into a field that belonged to Boaz, the relative of Naomi.

When Boaz saw her he said, "Whose daughter is this?" One of his servants told Boaz that she was the Moabite daughter-in-law of Naomi. Then Ruth said, "I pray you, let me glean and gather after the reapers among the sheaves." Boaz told her to stay in his field and not to glean in any other field. He wanted her to glean with his maidens. He also told her she might drink of the water that the young men had drawn.

Ruth could not understand the kindness of Boaz to her. Boaz told her that he had heard of Ruth's kindness to Naomi. He had heard how she had left her own father and mother, and had come to a people whom she did not know. Boaz was helpful to Ruth and Naomi.

Ruth went along with the other maidens of Boaz every workday to pick grain until the end of the harvest. In the evenings she would return with her grain to Naomi.

One day Boaz went to the gate of the city. There in the presence of ten witnesses he told the people that he had chosen Ruth to be his wife. The people were very much pleased to hear this. So Boaz and Ruth were married.

Boaz loved Ruth very much. They were happy together. After some time a baby boy was born to them. They called his name Obed. Obed was the grandfather of David, of whose line the Saviour was born.

QUESTIONS ON LESSON 11

1. *What do we know about Elimelech and Naomi?*
   Elimelech and Naomi were godly people who lived in Bethlehem.
2. *Where did Elimelech take his family because of a famine in Bethlehem?*
   Elimelech took his family to Moab.
3. *Whom did the two sons of Elimelech and Naomi marry in Moab?*
   The sons married two Moabite girls, Orpah and Ruth.
4. *What happened to this family after about ten years?*
   Elimelech and his two sons died.
5. *What did Orpah and Ruth do when Naomi returned to Bethlehem?*
   Ruth went with Naomi, but Orpah went back to her people.
6. *How did Ruth show that she really wanted to go with Naomi?*
   Ruth said, "Thy people shall be my people, and thy God my God."
7. *Whom did Ruth marry after she came to Bethlehem?*
   Ruth married Boaz, in whose fields she had gathered grain.

Exercise 1 (True or False)

1. Elimelech took his family to Moab because of a flood. _____.
   (Ruth 1:1)
2. Mahlon and Chilion married women of Israel. _____
3. Ruth decided to leave her own people to go with Naomi. _____
   (Ruth 1:16)
4. Orpah married Boaz, a relative of Elimelech. _____

Exercise 2 (Fill in Blanks)

1. "Orpah _____ her mother-in-law, but _____ clave unto her." (Ruth 1:14)
2. Ruth said, "Thy _____ shall be my _____ and thy God my _____." (Ruth 1:16)
3. Ruth gathered grain in the fields of _____. (Ruth 2:3)
4. Obed, the son of Boaz and Ruth, was the grandfather of _____ (Ruth 4:17)

Something to Think About

1. Did Elimelech do wisely in taking his family to Moab?
2. Israel was God's chosen people. Was Ruth an Israelite? (Ruth 1:4)
3. Can you figure out how Ruth became a relative to the Saviour? (Ruth 4:13-22)

Memory Verse: Matthew 10:37a.
He that loveth father or mother more than me is not worthy of me.

37

Lesson 12

SAMUEL, THE BOY

Read: 1 Samuel 1-4

While a priest named Eli ruled Israel, there lived a man named Elkanah. He was a kind and a good man. He had two wives, as was the custom of many men at that time. The name of the one was Hannah, and the name of the other was Peninnah.

Peninnah had children, but Hannah had no children. This made Hannah very sad. She wanted a little baby boy so much. Peninnah often teased Hannah because she had no children. This made Hannah even more sad. Elkanah, her husband, tried to comfort her; but she would not be comforted.

Once a year Elkanah and his family went to Shiloh, about fifteen miles away. They went to worship God in the tabernacle. On one of these visits Hannah prayed most earnestly to God for a baby son. Hannah knew that she should bring her needs to God. She also knew that God was able to help her. Hannah promised God that if He would give her a son, she would give him back to God to be used in His service. Eli saw Hannah praying in the temple and told her that God had heard her prayer and would give her a son. Hannah went home feeling very happy.

God did answer Hannah's prayer. Some time after this God gave Hannah a baby boy. She named him "Samuel," which means, "asked of God."

Hannah did not forget her promise to God. When Samuel was about three years old Hannah brought him to the temple. She told Eli, the priest, that she was the woman who had prayed for a son, and that God had answered her prayer. She also told Eli that she had promised to give the child back to God. Hannah wanted Samuel to live with Eli and to grow up in the house of God. Then Hannah praised God for His goodness.

Hannah returned home, leaving Samuel in the care of Eli. Each year when Hannah came to the tabernacle to worship she brought Samuel a new linen coat. God was very good to Hannah and gave her three more sons and two daughters.

Samuel lived with Eli in God's house. Every day he helped Eli. He took care of the lamps, and opened the doors of the tabernacle. Samuel was a good boy and obeyed Eli, the priest.

Eli had two sons who were also priests and who also worked in the tabernacle. But they were very wicked sons. Eli had not corrected them, as he should have when they were young. Now that the sons were grown they would not listen to their father Eli. These sons caused Eli much grief.

One night little Samuel went to bed as usual. After Samuel had fallen asleep, he heard a voice calling, "Samuel, Samuel!" Samuel thought it was Eli calling. He arose quickly and ran to Eli, saying, "Here am I, for thou calledst me." But Eli said, "I called not, my son, lie down again." So Samuel went back to his bed. Soon Samuel heard the voice again: "Samuel, Samuel!" Again he arose and ran to Eli, saying, "Here am I, for thou didst call me." But once again Eli said, "I called not, my son."

Soon Samuel heard the voice calling the third time: "Samuel, Samuel!" A third time he ran to Eli and said, "Here am I; for thou didst call me." Now Eli realized it must be God who was calling Samuel. So Eli told Samuel to lie down again. He told him that if he heard the voice again he should say, "Speak, Lord, for thy servant heareth." Then Samuel went back to bed once more. Soon the voice called again: "Samuel, Samuel!" Then Samuel answered, "Speak; for thy servant heareth." Then the Lord spoke to Samuel and gave him a message for Eli. He told Samuel that Eli's wicked sons were to be killed because they did not obey God.

Samuel lay in his bed until morning. In the morning he went about his work as usual. He was afraid to tell Eli what God had said. Then Eli called Samuel and said, "What is the thing that the Lord hath said unto thee?" Then Samuel told Eli all that God had said. And Eli said, "It is the Lord: let Him do what seemeth Him good."

Later, when the Israelites were at war with the Philistines, the two wicked sons of Eli were killed in one day. On that same day the Philistines captured the Ark of the Covenant. When Eli heard the report that his two sons were killed in battle and that the ark of the Lord was taken, he fell from his chair and broke his neck and died. So God punished Eli for failing to correct his sons. He punished the sons also for their great wickedness.

Then Samuel became the prophet of God to Israel.

QUESTIONS ON LESSON 12

1. *How did God answer Hannah's prayer?*
   God gave Hannah a son whom she named Samuel.
2. *What had Hannah promised the Lord in her prayer?*
   Hannah had promised that she would give the child back to God.
3. *Where did Hannah take Samuel when he was about three years old?*
   Hannah took Samuel to the temple for God's service.
4. *Who was Eli?*
   Eli was a God-fearing priest who had two wicked sons.
5. *What message did God give to Samuel one night?*
   God told Samuel that He was going to punish Eli and his sons.
6. *What shocking news did Eli receive after the battle with the Philistines?*
   A messenger told Eli that the Ark of God had been taken, and that his two sons had been killed.
7. *What happened to Eli when he heard this terrible news?*
   Eli fell off his seat backward, and died.

Exercise 1 (True or False)

1. Hannah prayed for a son in her old age. _____ (1 Sam. 1:10, 11)
2. Hannah called her son Samson. _____ (1 Sam. 1:20)
3. Samuel worked for Elijah in the temple. _____ (1 Sam. 2:11)
4. God spoke to Samuel while he was working in the temple. _____
   (1 Sam. 3:3, 4)

Exercise 2 (Fill in Blanks)

1. Hannah said to Eli, "For this child I _____. (1 Sam. 1:27)
2. Hannah made Samuel a little _____ for God's service.
   (1 Sam. 2:19)
3. God called Samuel and he answered, "_____ _____ ___."
   (1 Sam. 3:4)
4. Samuel said to the Lord, "Speak; for thy _____ heareth."
   (1 Sam. 3:10)

Something to Think About

1. Can you give any reason why Hannah prayed for a son? Why not for a daughter?
2. Is there any comparison in the New Testament to Hannah's song of thanksgiving? (Compare with Luke 1:46)
3. Why was the capture of the ark of God considered such a great loss?

Memory Verse: Psalm 91:15.
He shall call upon me, and I will answer him.

40

Lesson 13

ISRAEL'S FIRST KING

Read: 1 Samuel 8-10

Samuel was a good and wise judge. He judged Israel for many years. When he became old he made his sons judges in Israel. But Samuel's sons did not walk in their father's ways. Samuel was honest, but his sons were dishonest. They judged in favour of the person who would give them the most money.

One day the leaders of Israel came to Samuel. They said to him, "Behold, thou art old, and thy sons walk not in thy ways: now make us a king to judge us like all the nations."

Samuel was displeased with the request of the leaders. The people were forgetting that God was their king. Samuel prayed to the Lord about this. God said to Samuel, "Hearken unto the voice of the people in all that they say unto thee: for they have not rejected thee, but they have rejected me, that I should not reign over them."

The Lord told Samuel to give Israel a king. He also told Samuel to tell Israel what a king would be like. Samuel told Israel that their king would take the best of their children, and the best of their fields, and their vineyards and olive groves for himself. But the people wanted a king anyway. They said, "Nay, but we will have a king over us." The Lord said to Samuel, "Hearken unto their voice, and make them a king." Then Samuel sent all the people to their homes.

There was in the tribe of Benjamin a mighty man named Kish. He had a good-looking son named Saul. There was no man in Israel as handsome as Saul. He was a head taller than any other man in Israel.

One day some of the donkeys of Kish were lost. Kish said to Saul, "Take now one of thy servants with thee, and arise, go seek the donkeys." Saul and the servant looked throughout all the land, but they could not find them. After three days of searching they decided to return home. They were afraid Saul's father would worry about them.

The servant remembered that in the city nearby there was a man of God. The servant said, "He is an honourable man; all that he saith shall surely come to pass: now let us go thither; peradventure he can show us the way that we should go."

A day before this, God had said to Samuel, "Tomorrow, about this time, I will send thee a man out of the land of Benjamin, and thou shalt anoint him to be captain over my people Israel; that he may save my people out of the hand of the Philistines: for I have looked upon my people, because their cry is come unto Me."

As Saul and his servant came to the city they asked some young girls where the prophet was. These girls told them where they could find Samuel. Soon Saul and his servant met Samuel as he was going up to sacrifice. When Samuel saw Saul, God told him that this was the man who was to be king over Israel. Saul went to Samuel and said, "Tell me, I pray thee, where the seer's house is."

Samuel answered, "I am the seer: go up before me unto the high place; for ye shall eat with me today, and tomorrow I will let thee go, and will tell thee all that is in thine heart. And as for thy donkeys that were lost three days ago, set not thy mind on them; for they are found. And on whom is all the desire of Israel? Is it not on thee, and on all thy father's house?"

Saul said to Samuel, "Am not I a Benjamite, of the smallest of the tribes of Israel? and my family the least of all the families of the tribe of Benjamin? wherefore speakest thou so to me?" Then Samuel took Saul with him to the sacrifice. He was given the seat of honour. The best food was placed before him. That evening Saul went along with Samuel to his home.

Early in the morning Samuel awoke Saul and his servant and sent them on their way home. As Samuel was walking along with Saul he told him to send his servant on ahead. Samuel and Saul stood still. When the servant had gone on, Samuel kissed Saul and poured a bottle of oil upon his head. Samuel told Saul that the Lord had anointed him king of Israel.

After this Samuel called all the people to Mizpeh. There Samuel pointed out Saul as Israel's new king. Samuel said to all the people, "See ye him whom the Lord has chosen, that there is none like him among all the people?" Then all the people shouted, "God save the king."

QUESTIONS ON LESSON 13

1. *In what way were Samuel's sons different from their God-fearing father?*
   Samuel's sons were wicked and did not walk in their father's ways.
2. *What did the Lord say to Samuel when Israel asked for a king?*
   God said, "They have not rejected thee, but they have rejected me."
3. *How did Samuel try to discourage the people when they asked for a king?*
   Samuel told the Israelites that a king would be very demanding.
4. *What did the people of Israel say when Samuel told them God's words?*
   The people said, "Nay, but we will have a king over us."
5. *What did the Lord tell Samuel to do about Israel's request?*
   The Lord said to Samuel, "Hearken unto their voice, and make them a king."
6. *Whom did God choose to be king of Israel?*
   God chose Saul to be Israel's first king.
7. *How was Saul made king?*
   At God's command Samuel anointed Saul with oil.

Exercise 1 (True or False)

1. Samuel's sons walked in their father's ways. _____ (1 Sam. 8:3)
2. Samuel was ready to give Israel a king. _____ (1 Sam. 8:6)
3. God was pleased that Israel asked for a king. _____ (1 Sam. 8:7)
4. God chose Saul to be Israel's king. _____.

Exercise 2 (Fill in Blanks)

1. Kish had a son whose name was _____. (1 Sam. 9:1-2)
2. Samuel took a vial of _____ and poured it upon Saul's head. (1 Sam. 10:1)
3. Samuel said. "See ye him whom the _____ hath chosen." (1 Sam. 10:24)
4. All the people said, "God _____ the king." (1 Sam. 10:24)

Something to Think About

1. Who was the king of Israel before Saul?
2. What was the purpose of the anointing oil in making Saul king? (1 Sam. 10:1)
3. What three signs did God give Saul to make him feel sure that God had chosen him to be Israel's king? (1 Sam. 10:1-7)

Memory Verse: 1 Samuel 8:7.
They have not rejected thee, but they have rejected Me.

Lesson 14

GOD CHOOSES A NEW KING FOR ISRAEL

Read: 1 Samuel 16

King Saul was a good king at first. But he soon became proud, and disobedient to God. Because of this Samuel told Saul that the Lord was going to take the kingdom from him and give it to another.

The old prophet Samuel felt very sorry for Saul. One day the Lord asked Samuel why he kept on feeling sad about Saul. The Lord said, "I have rejected him from reigning over Israel." The Lord told Samuel to fill his horn with oil and go to Jesse in Bethlehem. God had chosen a king for Israel from one of Jesse's sons.

Samuel said, "How can I go? If Saul hear it, he will kill me." The Lord said to Samuel, "Take a heifer with thee, and say, I am come to sacrifice to the Lord. And call Jesse to the sacrifice, and I will show thee what thou shalt do: and thou shalt anoint unto me him whom I name unto thee."

Samuel obeyed the Lord. He went to Jesse's home in Bethlehem. When the elders of the city saw the prophet coming they were afraid. They said, "Comest thou peaceably?" Samuel told them that he came peaceably. He told them that he wished to sacrifice to the Lord.

Then Samuel called Jesse and his sons to the sacrifice. When they had gathered around the altar, Samuel asked Jesse's sons to walk past him. Eliab, the oldest son, came first. He was a very tall and handsome young man. He looked as if he would make a good king. Samuel thought surely Eliab would be God's choice. But God said, "Look not on his countenance, or on the height of his stature; because I have refused him: for the Lord seeth not as man seeth; for man looketh on the outward appearance, but the Lord looketh on the heart."

One by one the seven sons of Jesse passed before Samuel. But God did not choose any of them. Then Samuel said to Jesse, "Are here all thy children?" And Jesse said, "There remaineth yet the youngest, and, behold, he keepeth the sheep." Samuel said to Jesse, "Send and fetch him: for we will not sit down till he come hither."

Right away they sent for David and brought him in. Then the Lord said to Samuel "Arise, anoint him, for this is he." Samuel took his horn of oil and anointed him to be the king of Israel. Then the Spirit of the

Lord came into David's heart. After the sacrifice David went back to the sheep. Samuel went to Ramah.

David grew up strong and brave. He was not afraid of the wild beasts that tried to steal and destroy his sheep. Once he killed a bear, and at another time he killed a lion.

As David took care of his sheep he had much time to think about God and to pray. David was a musician. He loved to play his harp. He also wrote some beautiful songs, which we know as the Psalms. One of the songs he wrote is the Twenty-third Psalm. This is often called the Shepherd Psalm. It begins with the words, "The Lord is my shepherd."

The Spirit of God was making David strong for God's service. At the same time God's Spirit was leaving Saul. He became more and more disobedient to God. There were times when an evil spirit troubled Saul.

One of Saul's servants had heard of Jesse's son, David. He told Saul many nice things about David. He told Saul that David was a good musician, a good warrior, a wise man, a good-looking man, and best of all he said, "And the Lord is with him."

Saul sent messengers to bring David to the palace. Jesse was willing to let David go. He sent a good present along for the king.

Whenever the evil spirit troubled Saul, he would ask David to play his harp for him. This made Saul feel better again and the evil spirit would go away from him.

Saul had three sons and two daughters. One of the sons was named Jonathan. David and Jonathan became good friends. They loved each other like brothers.

QUESTIONS ON LESSON 14

1. *How did Saul show that he was not a good king?*
   Saul became proud and disobedient to God.
2. *What did the Lord say when Samuel felt sad about Saul?*
   The Lord said, "I have rejected him from reigning over Israel."
3. *How did God provide a king to take Saul's place?*
   God chose a king from among the sons of Jesse.
4. *How did Samuel go about making David the king of Israel?*
   Samuel anointed David in the presence of his father and brothers.
5. *In what way did Saul show that he became less fit to be a king?*
   God's Spirit left Saul and an evil spirit troubled him.
6. *What did David do for Saul when the evil spirit came upon him?*
   David played his harp and Saul felt much better.

Exercise 1 (True or False)

1. Saul was obedient to the Lord all his life. _____
2. Samuel was afraid to anoint a king in Saul's stead. _____
   (1 Sam. 16:2)
3. Samuel thought Eliab would make a good king. _____ (1 Sam. 16:6)
4. When David was anointed king, God's Spirit came upon him. _____
   (1 Sam. 16:13)

Exercise 2 (Fill in Blanks)

1. God sent Samuel to the home of _____ to anoint a new king.
   (1 Sam. 16:1)
2. Samuel said, "If Saul hear it, he will _____ me." (1 Sam. 16:2)
3. God chose David, Jesse's _____ son, to be the king.
   (1 Sam. 16:11, 12)
4. When the evil spirit troubled Saul, David played his _____.

Something to Think About

1. Why did the elders of Bethlehem tremble at Samuel's coming?
   (1 Sam. 16:4)
2. How do you think Saul acted when the evil spirit troubled him?
   (1 Sam. 18:10)
3. Why did Saul feel better when David played his harp?
4. What kind of songs do you think he played?

Memory Verse: 1 Samuel 16:7.
For man looketh on the outward appearance, but the Lord looketh on the heart.

46

Lesson 15

DAVID KILLS THE GIANT GOLIATH

Read: 1 Samuel 17

While Saul was still king, the Philistines again made war upon the Israelites. The Philistine army was on one mountain and Saul's army was on another mountain. There was a valley between the two armies.

Each day a giant came out of the Philistine camp. His name was Goliath. He was a great warrior. He was at least nine feet tall. He wore a helmet of brass, and a coat of steel upon his shoulders. His legs were protected by plates of brass, and he carried a big spear. He had a shield-bearer to go before him.

Each day this giant warrior would walk up and down the valley. Then he would dare some one of Israel's army to come out and fight with him. Then the giant boasted, "I defy the armies of Israel this day: give me a man, that we may fight together." When Saul and his army heard Goliath's loud voice and his terrible words, they were very much afraid. No one dared to fight Goliath. Every day for forty days the giant came out and challenged the Israelites.

David's three oldest brothers were in Saul's army, but David had returned to his home to feed his sheep at Bethlehem. One day Jesse sent David to visit his three brothers, and to bring them a present.

As David was talking to his brothers, the giant Goliath came out again. As always, he called for someone to come out and fight with him. David heard what Goliath said. He also saw that whenever the giant came out, the Israelites fled from him.

David heard the Israelites talk about the great rewards the king had promised to anyone who would kill the giant. David asked about this giant. He was surprised that anyone dared to speak so proudly against God's people.

When Saul heard of David he sent for him. David said to Saul, "Let no man's heart fail because of him: thy servant will go and fight this Philistine."

David told Saul that when he was caring for his father's sheep a lion and a bear came and took a lamb out of the flock. David said, "Thy servant slew both the lion and the bear; and this uncircumcised Philistine shall be as one of them, seeing he hath defied the armies of the living God."

David also said, "The Lord that delivered me out of the paw of the lion, and out of the paw of the bear, he will deliver me out of the hand of this Philistine." And Saul said to David, "Go, and the Lord be with thee."

Saul tried to put his armour on David and to fit him for the battle. But David could not go in Saul's armour; it was too big and so he took it off. David took his staff in his hand and his sling. As he walked toward the giant he picked up five smooth stones out of the brook. He put them into his shepherd's bag.

When Goliath saw David coming, he said, "Am I a dog, that thou comest to me with staves?... Come to me, and I will give thy flesh to the fowls of the air, and to the beasts of the field."

Then David said, "Thou comest to me with a sword, and with a spear, and with a shield: but I come to thee in the name of the Lord of hosts, the God of the armies of Israel, whom thou hast defied."

As Goliath came forward, David shot one of the stones from his slingshot. The stone sank deep into the giant's forehead, and Goliath fell upon his face to the earth. Quickly David drew out the giant's big sword, and cut off his head with it.

When the Philistines saw that Goliath was dead they fled. The Israelites chased the Philistines to the city of Gath and killed many of them. God gave the Israelites a great victory that day.

After David had killed the giant Goliath he stayed at the palace. The people of Israel honoured David more than their king Saul. This made Saul jealous and twice he tried to kill David.

God did not bless Saul anymore like He did at first. Saul was disobedient to God and since Samuel was dead, he did not know where to go for help. One day he even went to a witch for advice, but that only made matters worse.

After some time the Philistines again came to fight with the Israelites. It was a terrible battle. Both Saul and his son Jonathan were killed. After this David became king over Israel.

QUESTIONS ON LESSON 15

1. *Who was Goliath?*
   Goliath was a Philistine giant who defied God and His people.
2. *Where was David at this time?*
   David was taking care of his father's sheep.
3. *Where did Jesse send David?*
   Jesse sent David to visit his three brothers in Saul's army.
4. *What did David do when he heard Goliath's boast?*
   David told Saul that he was willing to fight the giant.
5. *What made David think that he could fight Goliath?*
   David trusted that God would help him.
6. *How did David fight the giant?*
   David killed the giant with a stone from his slingshot.
7. *What did the Philistines do when they saw their warrior was dead?*
   The Philistines fled, but the Israelites destroyed many of them.

Exercise 1 (True or False)

1. The Israelites were not afraid of the Philistines. _____
2. No Israelite dared to fight the giant Goliath. _____ (1 Sam. 17:11)
3. David trusted in his slingshot to kill Goliath. _____ (1 Sam. 17:37)

Exercise 2 (Fill in Blanks)

1. David said, "Thy servant will go and _____ with this Philistine." (1 Sam. 17:32)
2. David "choose him five smooth _____ out of the _____. (1 Sam. 17:40)
3. Goliath said, "Am I a _____, that thou comest to me with _____?" (1 Sam. 17:43)
4. David took Goliath's _____ and cut off his _____ with it." (1 Sam. 17:51)

Something to Think About

1. Did the Israelites believe in the same God as David?
2. Try to think of the many ways in which God prepared David for the throne.

Memory Verse: Psalm 71:16a.
I will go in the strength of the Lord God.

Lesson 16

SOLOMON, THE WISE KING

Read: 2 Samuel 18; 1 Kings 1-11; 2 Chronicles 1-9

David was a good king and a great warrior. As soon as the kings of other nations saw that Israel had a strong king, they made war against Israel. But God was with David in his battles.

David had many sons. His son Absalom was a wicked man. He made plans to take the throne away from his father David. Suddenly one day, the news was spread by swift runners, "Absalom reigneth in Hebron." David quickly escaped from the palace with his family. After some time a great battle was fought between those who followed Absalom and the soldiers of David. David's men killed many of Absalom's soldiers. When Absalom tried to flee on his mule from David's men he rode under the thick boughs of an oak tree. His head caught in the branches of the tree, and his mule ran from under him. While he was hanging there one of David's men shot three darts into Absalom's heart. That day Absalom was killed. This made David very sad.

King David had another son whose name was Solomon. He was not wicked like Absalom. Solomon was the man whom God had chosen to be the king after David.

When David was old, Solomon was anointed to be the next king. David's servants set Solomon on the king's mule to ride through the city. David was very happy that Solomon was to be the king after him. He said, "He shall be king in my stead: and I have appointed him to be ruler over Israel and over Judah." As the people saw Solomon riding on the king's mule they blew their trumpets and shouted, "God save king Solomon." Before king David died he blessed his son Solomon. He warned Solomon to walk in the ways of God's holy Word.

Solomon was a good king like his father David. One day he went to Gibeon to offer a thousand burnt offerings to God on the altar there. That night God came to Solomon in a dream saying, "Ask what I shall give thee."

Solomon was greatly surprised at this. Then Solomon said, "O Lord my God, thou hast made thy servant king instead of David my father: and I am but a little child: I know not how to go out or to come in. And thy servant is in the midst of thy people which thou hast chosen, a great people, which cannot be counted. Give therefore thy servant an understanding heart to judge thy people that I may discern between good and bad."

God was very much pleased with Solomon's choice. He had not asked for long life and riches, or other things for himself. Because Solomon had made this choice, God promised to give Solomon a wise and understanding heart. Solomon would have greater wisdom than any man that had ever lived, or was ever going to live. God also promised Solomon great riches and honour.

One day Solomon's wisdom was put to the test. He had to judge between two young women. Each of them had a little baby boy. During the night one of the babies had died. In the morning each claimed the living baby to be her own.

Solomon thought about this for a while. Then he said, "Bring me a sword." When they brought it he said, "Divide the living child in two, and give half to the one, and half to the other." Then the living baby's mother said, "O my lord, give her the living child, and in no wise slay it." But the other said, "Let it be neither mine nor thine, but divide it." Solomon saw who was the real mother. She was the one who loved the baby and did not want it to be killed.

Solomon built a most beautiful temple for the Lord. It took him seven years to complete the building. He had thirty thousand Jews working on it and one hundred fifty-three thousand, six hundred Canaanites. The temple was built on Mount Moriah, the highest place in the land. God Himself gave Solomon the plans for the building of the temple. It was built after the general plan of the tabernacle, Israel's tent-church. Neither hammer nor axe, nor any tool of iron was heard while they built the temple. All the parts were made ready at a distance and then brought in to be put together quietly. Much gold was used in this building. It is said that the building would cost from two to five billion dollars in our money.

God gave Solomon great riches and honour. People came from far and near to see Solomon's kingdom. But when he became old he made a great mistake. He married many heathen wives who drew his heart away from the Lord. They brought idol worship into Solomon's kingdom. This was displeasing to the Lord who had so wonderfully blessed him.

QUESTIONS ON LESSON 16

1. *How did God show that He was with David?*
   God helped David to conquer many nations.
2. *In what way did David's son Absalom show his wickedness?*
   Absalom tried to take the throne away from his father.
3. *How did Absalom come to a sad end?*
   Absalom was killed.
4. *Who became king in David's place?*
   Solomon became king after his father David.
5. *What did Solomon ask of the Lord?*
   Solomon asked the Lord for an understanding heart.
6. *How did Solomon show his great love for God?*
   Solomon built a beautiful temple for the Lord's service.
7. *What sad thing happened in Solomon's old age?*
   Solomon's many heathen wives turned his heart after other gods.

Exercise 1 (True or False)

1. Absalom asked the Lord for an understanding heart. _____
2. The Lord promised Solomon great riches and honour. _____
   (1 Kings 3:13)
3. Solomon built a beautiful temple for God's service. _____
   (1 Kings 6)
4. Many heathen wives drew Solomon's heart away from the
   Lord. _____ (1 Kings 11:1-13)

Exercise 2 (Fill in Blanks)

1. Absalom tried to take the _____ from his father David.
2. Absalom's head caught in the branches of a tree and his _____
   went away.
3. Solomon became _____ in his father's stead. (1 Kings 1:30)
4. Solomon asked the Lord for an understanding _____.
   (1 Kings 3:9)

Something to Think About

1. Do you think Absalom would have made a good king?
2. What do you understand by "A wise and understanding heart"?
3. Did Solomon's great wisdom make him "sin-proof"?

Memory Verse: Proverbs 3:5.
Trust in the Lord with all thine heart;
and lean not unto thine own understanding.

Lesson 17

GOD'S PROPHET ELIJAH

Read: 2 Chronicles 10; 1 Kings 12-17

When Solomon died, his son Rehoboam became king. Some of the people were displeased with him. They followed a man named Jeroboam. Only the tribes of Judah and Benjamin were loyal to Rehoboam.

Jeroboam was king over ten tribes. He made two calves of gold. One he placed at Bethel and the other at Dan. Then he said to the people, "It is too much for you to go up to Jerusalem: behold thy gods, O Israel, which brought thee up out of the land of Egypt." In this way Jeroboam brought idol worship to Israel and the people worshipped false gods.

There was war between Rehoboam and Jeroboam as long as they lived. Rehoboam ruled over the kingdom of Judah, and Jeroboam ruled over the kingdom of Israel.

After Jeroboam's death other wicked kings ruled over the kingdom of Israel. In time Omri became king. While he was king over Israel he bought a hill for two talents of silver. He built a city on this hill and called it Samaria. It was named after Shemer, the man who had owned the hill before. But Omri was more wicked than all the kings before him. When he died his wicked son Ahab became king. He married Jezebel, a wicked Zidonian woman. Ahab followed her wicked ways, worshipping idols and building altars to them.

In those days of great sin and idol-worship there lived a prophet of God in Gilead. His name was Elijah. One day Elijah went to Ahab with a message from God. He said to the king, "As the Lord God of Israel liveth, before whom I stand, there shall not be dew nor rain these years, but according to my word."

For three years and six months it did not rain. No dew fell upon the ground during that time. As a result crops would not grow. There was no grass or food for the cattle and sheep. There was very little food for the people. The Lord knew that this would make Ahab very angry. God told Elijah to flee and to hide himself by the brook Cherith. This little stream was in the wilderness near Jericho. There God made big birds, called ravens, bring Elijah bread and meat every morning and every evening. He drank water from the brook.

After a while, the brook dried up. There had been no rain for a long time. Then the Lord said to Elijah, "Arise, get thee to Zarephath, and dwell there: behold, I have commanded a widow woman there to sustain thee." So Elijah went to Zarephath. When he came to the gate of the city there was a widow gathering sticks. Elijah called to her and said, "Fetch me, I pray thee, a little water in a vessel, that I may drink." As she was going he called to her, and said, "Bring me, I pray thee, a morsel of bread in thine hand."

The woman said to Elijah, "As the Lord thy God liveth, I have not a cake, but an handful of meal in a barrel, and a little oil in a cruse: and, behold I am gathering two sticks, that I may go in and dress it for me and my son, that we may eat it, and die."

Elijah said to the woman, "Fear not, go and do as thou hast said: but make me thereof a little cake first, and bring it unto me, and after make for thee and for thy son." Then Elijah added, "For thus saith the Lord God of Israel. The barrel of meal shall not waste, neither shall the cruse of oil fail, until the day that the Lord sendeth rain upon the earth."

The widow went and obeyed Elijah. She and her son, and Elijah had food for many days. There was always meal left in the barrel and oil enough in the cruse.

One day the widow's son became sick. Soon he became very seriously ill and died. Then the widow said to Elijah, "O thou man of God, art thou come unto me to bring my sin to remembrance, and to slay my son?" And Elijah said to her, "Give me thy son." Elijah carried the boy to his upstairs room. He laid the boy on the bed. Then he cried to the Lord, "O Lord my God, hast thou also brought evil upon the widow with whom I sojourn, by slaying her son?"

Then Elijah stretched himself upon the body of the boy three times. Elijah prayed to the Lord again. He said, "O Lord my God, I pray thee, let this child's soul come into him again." The Lord heard and answered Elijah's prayer. God gave the soul back to the body, and the boy lived again. Elijah took the boy and brought him to his mother saying, "See, thy son liveth."

The woman said to Elijah, "Now by this I know that thou art a man of God, and that the word of the Lord in thy mouth is truth."

QUESTIONS ON LESSON 17

1. *Who became king of Israel after Solomon's death?*
   Rehoboam became king in his father's stead.
2. *What did some of the tribes do when Rehoboam became king?*
   Ten tribes followed a man named Jeroboam.
3. *What wicked thing did Jeroboam do?*
   Jeroboam made two golden calves for Israel to worship.
4. *Who was Ahab?*
   Ahab was one of the most wicked kings of Israel.
5. *What did the prophet Elijah tell wicked king Ahab?*
   Elijah told Ahab that God would not send rain for a long time.
6. *How did God protect Elijah from Ahab's anger?*
   God told Elijah to hide himself by the brook Cherith.
7. *How did God provide food and drink for Elijah?*
   Ravens brought Elijah bread and meat, and he drank water from the brook.

Exercise 1 (True or False)

1. All the tribes of Israel gladly followed king Rehoboam. _____
   (1 Kings 12:17, 19)
2. Jeroboam led the Israelites to worship idols. _____
   (1 Kings 12:28-33)
3. Ahab was a very wicked king. _____ (1 Kings 16:30)
4. God sent the prophet Elijah to Jeroboam. _____ (1 Kings 17:1)

Exercise 2 (Fill in Blanks)

1. Elijah told Ahab that God would not send _____ for a long time.
   (1 Kings 17:1)
2. When Ahab became angry, Elijah hid by the _____ Cherith.
   (1 Kings 17:3)
3. The ravens brought Elijah _____ and _____.
   (1 Kings 17:6)
4. God provided food for Elijah and a widow and her _____.
   (1 Kings 17:15)

Something to Think About

1. Why did God hold back the rain from Israel when king Ahab was so wicked?
2. Why did God use a widow to help Elijah? Why not a rich man?
3. Can you see God's mercy towards Israel in spite of the lack of rain?

Memory Verse: Psalm 115:3.
But our God is in the heavens; he hath done whatsoever he hath pleased.

Lesson 18

GOD ANSWERS ELIJAH'S PRAYER
BY FIRE AND RAIN

Read: 1 Kings 18

Three years passed by. In all that time no rain fell upon the land of Israel. Crops would not grow. It was hard to find grass for the cattle and flocks. There was very little food for the people.

In the third year God said to Elijah, "Go, show thyself unto Ahab; and I will send rain upon the earth." When Ahab saw Elijah he said to him, "Art thou he that troubleth Israel?" Elijah answered, "I have not troubled Israel, but thou, and thy father's house, in that ye have forsaken the commandments of the Lord and thou hast followed Baalim."

Then Elijah told Ahab to gather all the people of Israel and the prophets of Baal on Mount Carmel. When all the people were gathered together on the mountain, Elijah said to the people, "How long halt ye between two opinions? if the Lord be God, follow Him: but if Baal then follow him."

Again Elijah spoke to the people saying, "Let them therefore give us two bullocks: and let them choose one bullock for themselves, and cut it in pieces, and lay it on the wood, and put no fire under it: and I will dress the other bullock, and lay it on wood, and put no fire under. And call ye on the name of your gods, and I will call on the name of the Lord: and the God that answereth by fire, let him be God." And all the people said, "It is well spoken."

Elijah asked the prophets to prepare their offering first. When their offering was ready they cried to their god saying, "O Baal, hear us." But there was no answer. From morning till noon they cried to their god. Finally, they jumped upon the altar, but received no answer.

Elijah mocked them saying, "Cry aloud; for he is a god; either he is talking or he is pursuing, or he is in a journey, or peradventure he sleepeth, and must be awaked." The prophets cried loudly and wildly. They cut themselves with knives till the blood spurted out. The middle of the afternoon came. Still Baal had not answered or sent fire upon the sacrifice.

Finally Elijah said to the people, "Come near unto me." All the people came near to him. Elijah then took twelve stones, one for each tribe of Israel. With these he rebuilt the broken down altar of the Lord. Then Elijah made a trench around the altar. He placed the wood upon the altar. He cut the bullock in pieces and placed it upon the wood. Then Elijah commanded the people to take four barrels of water and pour the water upon the altar. He told them to do it the second time and the third time. The altar, the wood and the sacrifice were soaked with water. The water ran round about the altar. Even the trench was filled with water.

At the time of the evening sacrifice Elijah prayed to God saying, "Lord God of Abraham, Isaac, and of Israel, let it be known this day that Thou art God in Israel, and that I am Thy servant, and that I have done all these things at Thy word. Hear, me, O Lord, hear me, that this people may know that Thou art the Lord God, and that Thou hast turned their heart back again."

Then God sent down fire from heaven, and burned up the offering, the wood, and also the stones and the dust. It even licked up the water that was in the trench. When the people saw it they said, "The Lord, he is the God; the Lord, he is the God."

At Elijah's command the people took the four hundred fifty prophets of Baal and brought them to the brook Kishon. There Elijah killed all these wicked prophets.

Then Elijah said to king Ahab, "Get thee up, eat and drink; for there is a sound of abundance of rain." While Ahab was eating and drinking, Elijah was praying upon Mount Carmel. He asked the Lord to send rain. After a while Elijah sent his servant to the top of the mountain to look toward the sea. The servant came back to Elijah and said, "There is nothing."

The servant went to look seven times. When he returned the seventh time he said, "Behold, there ariseth a little cloud out of the sea, like a man's hand." Then Elijah sent word to Ahab saying, "Prepare thy chariot, and get thee down, that the rain stop thee not." In the meanwhile the sky became black with clouds. The wind blew and there was a great rain. Ahab rode in his chariot to his palace at Jezreel. The power of the Lord came upon Elijah, and he ran ahead of Ahab's chariot to the gate of the city.

God answered Elijah's prayers by fire and rain. He proved that He is the only true and living God.

QUESTIONS ON LESSON 18

1. *For how long did God hold back the rain from Israel?*
   It did not rain for three years and six months.
2. *What did Elijah tell Ahab to do when he met him?*
   Elijah told Ahab to gather all the prophets of Baal at Mount Carmel.
3. *Why did Elijah want to gather all these wicked prophets?*
   God wanted to prove to the wicked prophets that He is God.
4. *What happened when the prophets cried to Baal?*
   Baal remained silent.
5. *How did God answer Elijah's prayer?*
   God sent fire from heaven upon Elijah's sacrifice.
6. *What did Elijah do to the wicked prophets of Baal?*
   Elijah killed the four hundred fifty prophets of Baal.
7. *What did Elijah do after he had killed the prophets?*
   Elijah prayed for rain and God sent abundant showers.

Exercise 1 (True or False)

1. Ahab worshipped the true God of Israel. _____
2. Baal was able to send fire upon the altar. _____
3. God's fire from heaven licked up the water in the trench. ____
4. God answered Elijah's prayer by sending rain. _____

Exercise 2 (Fill in Blanks)

1. Ahab said to. Elijah, "Art thou he that troubleth _____
   (1 Kings 18:17)
2. Elijah said, "How long _____ ye between _____ opinions."
   (1 Kings 18:21)
3. The wicked prophets cried, "O Baal, _____ us." (1 Kings 18:26)
4. God's fire licked up the _____ in the trench. (1 Kings 18:38)

Something to Think About

1. Did Ahab really believe that Elijah troubled Israel?
2. Could not Baal's prophets see that Baal was a dead idol?
3. Read what Psalm 115 tells us about idols.

Memory Verse: Psalm 113:5.
Who is like unto the Lord our God, who dwelleth on high?

Lesson 19

ELISHA IS GOD'S NEW PROPHET

Read: 1 Kings 19; 2 Kings 2

Elijah was a great prophet and he worked in Israel for many years. He warned the wicked kings, and taught the people to serve the true God instead of the idol Baal.

At last Elijah's work was to come to an end. God told Elijah that a man named Elisha would be prophet in his place. When Elijah went to look for Elisha, he found him plowing with twelve yoke of oxen before him. He was following the twelfth yoke. Elijah went up to him and threw his coat over Elisha. This meant that Elisha was to follow Elijah. So the young man left his work and followed Elijah.

At that time there were schools where young men were trained to be prophets. There were three of these schools: one at Gilgal, one at Bethel and one at Jericho.

Shortly before God was going to take Elijah up into heaven, Elijah went with Elisha to Gilgal. While at Gilgal, Elijah said to Elisha, "Tarry here, I pray thee, for the Lord hath sent me to Bethel." But Elisha said, "As the Lord liveth, and as thy soul liveth, I will not leave thee." So they both went to Bethel. At Bethel the sons of the prophets said to Elisha, "Knowest thou that the Lord will take away thy master today?" And he said, "Yea, I know it; hold ye your peace." While they were at Bethel Elijah said to Elisha, "Tarry here, I pray thee; for the Lord hath sent me to Jericho." And Elisha said, "As the Lord liveth, and as thy soul liveth, I will not leave thee." So they came to Jericho.

At Jericho the sons of the prophets came to Elisha saying, "Knowest thou that the Lord will take away your master today?" Here also Elisha answered, "Yea, I know it: hold ye your peace."

While at Jericho Elijah said to Elisha, "Tarry, I pray thee, here: for the Lord hath sent me to Jordan." And Elisha repeated, "As the Lord liveth, and as thy soul liveth, I will not leave thee." So both went on their way.

As the two prophets went on their way, fifty sons of the prophets stood watching them. When they came to the Jordan River, Elijah took his coat and wrapped it together. He hit the water with it. At once the water was parted. The two men crossed over on dry ground.

When they reached the other side, Elijah said to Elisha, "Ask what I shall do for thee." Elisha said to Elijah, "I pray thee, let a double portion of thy spirit be upon me."

Elijah said, "Thou hast asked a hard thing: nevertheless; if thou see me when I am taken from thee, it shall be so unto thee; but if not, it shall not be so." As they went on and talked, all at once the two men saw a fiery chariot drawn by fiery horses. It came between the two men and picked up Elijah. Elijah went up by a whirlwind into heaven. Elisha was so surprised. He cried, "My father, my father, the chariot of Israel, and the horsemen thereof." Elisha saw him no more. Then he tore his own clothes in two pieces. Very likely this was to show his grief.

Then Elisha took Elijah's coat, which had fallen from him, and went back to the Jordan River. He took Elijah's coat and hit the water with it as he had seen Elijah do. The path came in the water again. Elisha passed over on dry ground. This was proof that the spirit of Elijah had come upon Elisha. God had chosen Elisha to be his prophet.

When the sons of the prophets saw Elisha, they said, "The spirit of Elijah doth rest upon Elisha." While Elisha was staying at Jericho the men of the city came to Elisha. They said, "Behold, I pray thee, the situation of this city is pleasant, as my lord seeth; but the water is naught, and the ground barren."

Elisha said to them, "Bring me a new cruse, and put salt therein." The men brought the cruse and the salt to him. Elisha took the cruse of salt to the spring of water. He threw the salt into it. He said, "Thus saith the Lord, I have healed these waters; there shall not be from thence anymore death or barren land." And the waters were made useful by God.

From Jericho Elisha went to Bethel. As he was walking along, some youths made fun of him saying, "Go up, thou bald head; go up, thou bald head." Elisha turned back and cursed them in the name of the Lord. Then two bears came out of the woods and mauled forty-two of these wicked young men. This was God's way of saying, "Do my prophets no harm."

QUESTIONS ON LESSON 19

1. *Whom did God choose to become the prophet after Elijah?*
   God chose Elisha to become the prophet in Elijah's stead.
2. *What did Elijah do to show that Elisha was to follow him?*
   Elijah threw his coat upon Elisha.
3. *What happened when Elijah struck the water with his coat?*
   The waters of Jordan were divided, leaving a dry path.
4. *What happened when Elijah and Elisha were talking together?*
   God sent a chariot and horses of fire, and a whirlwind which took Elijah up to heaven.
5. *What did the children of Bethel say to Elijah?*
   The youths made fun of Elisha, saying, "Go up, thou bald head."
6. *How did the Lord punish these youths for despising His servant?*
   God sent two bears to maul the forty-two youths.

Exercise 1 (True or False)

1. When Elijah became old he died. _____
2. Elisha followed Elijah without saying goodbye to his parents. _____
   (1 Kings 19:20)
3. Elijah struck the waters of the Red Sea and they parted. _____
   (2 Kings 2:7, 8)
4. Elijah went up to heaven like Jesus did. _____. (2 Kings 2:11; Acts 1:9)

Exercise 2 (Fill in Blanks)

1. Elijah found Elisha in the field _____. (1 Kings 19:19)
2. Elisha asked for a double portion of Elijah's _____.
   (2 Kings 2:9)
3. Fifty men looked for Elijah for _____ days after he was gone.
   (2 Kings 2:16, 17)
4. God sent two she _____ to punish the wicked youths.
   (2 Kings 2:24)

Something to Think About

1. How wonderfully God provides for men who will speak for Him to God's people!
2. Can you prove from our Bible reading that Elijah's spirit came upon Elisha? (See 2 Kings 2:13-15.)
3. Did Elijah ever come back from heaven after God took him away? (See 2 Kings 2:16-18; Luke 9:28-36.)

Memory Verse: Romans 8:14.
For as many as are led by the Spirit of God, they are the sons of God.

Lesson 20

GOD HEALS NAAMAN OF LEPROSY

Read: 2 Kings 5

To the north of Israel lay the country of Syria. The king of Syria had a very good captain in his service. His name was Naaman. Naaman was highly honoured by the king and the people. He was a good soldier, and the Lord helped him to win many victories. But there was something very seriously wrong with Naaman. He was a leper, which was a very loathsome disease.

At the home of Naaman there was a little Hebrew slave girl. Even though Naaman and his wife did not know the true God they seemed to be kind to their maid. The little maid felt sorry for Naaman. She knew Israel's God and she knew of Elisha, God's prophet.

One day she said to Naaman's wife, "Would God my lord were with the prophet that is in Samaria! for he would recover him of his leprosy." These words were told to the king and surely caused a great stir in the palace. The king was ready to send Naaman to Israel right away. He said, to Naaman, "Go,... and I will send a letter unto the king of Israel." So Naaman left, and took with him expensive presents of gold and silver, and other precious things.

After travelling about one hundred miles, Naaman and his servants came to King Joram of Israel. Naaman brought the king's letter to the king of Israel. In the letter Joram read, "Behold, I have…sent Naaman my servant to thee, that thou mayest recover him of his leprosy." The king of Israel became so alarmed that he tore his clothes. He said, "Am I God, to kill and to make alive, that this man doth send unto me to recover a man of his leprosy? Wherefore consider, I pray you, and see how he seeketh a quarrel with me."

The prophet Elisha heard about the king's alarm at the letter that Naaman had brought. Elisha sent a message to the king, saying, "Wherefore hast thou rent thy clothes? let him come now to me, and he shall know that there is a prophet in Israel."

So Naaman came with his horses and chariot to Elisha. But Elisha did not even go to meet him. He sent his servant to Naaman, saying, "Go and wash in Jordan seven times, and thy flesh shall again come to thee, and thou shalt be clean." This made Naaman very angry. He thought the prophet would at least come and wave his hand over his leprosy and pray to God for him. He said, "Are not Abana and Pharpar, rivers of Damascus, better than all the waters of Israel? may I not wash in them and be clean?" So Naaman turned away very angry.

Then Naaman's servants said to him, "My father, if the prophet had bid thee do some great thing, wouldest thou not have done it? how much rather then, when he saith to thee, Wash, and be clean?" This cooled Naaman's anger and he decided to do as Elisha had said. Naaman dipped himself seven times in the Jordan River. His flesh became pure and pink as a child's. How happy Naaman was! Returning to Elisha, he said, "Behold, now I know that there is no God in all the earth, but in Israel." Naaman wanted Elisha to take a present from him. But Elisha refused to take it. He wanted Naaman to know that the Lord had healed him.

Then Naaman asked two favours of Elisha. The first one was whether he might take from Israel as much earth as two mules could carry. Naaman said, "Thy servant will henceforth offer neither burnt offering nor sacrifice unto other gods, but unto the Lord."

The second favour was this. When the king of Syria went into the temple of Rimmon, the king always leaned on Naaman's hand to bow before his idol. Then Naaman had to bend too. But Naaman wanted Elisha to know that by doing this he was not worshipping the idol. From now on he would worship only the true God. Elisha said, "Go in peace."

After this, Naaman left Elisha's house. When he was well on the way, Gehazi, Elisha's servant, remembered that Naaman had offered Elisha a present. He thought secretly, "Why don't I try to get this present for myself?" Quickly he went after Naaman. He told him that two sons of the prophets had just come, and he said, "Give them, I pray thee, a talent of silver, and two changes of garments."

Naaman was happy and ready to give him two talents of silver and the garments. Gehazi returned to Elisha secretly. But Elisha knew where his servant had been. He told Gehazi that as a punishment the leprosy of Naaman would cling to him. Gehazi went out from Elisha's house a leper. His flesh was white as snow.

QUESTIONS ON LESSON 20

1. *Who was Naaman?*
   Naaman was a captain in the Syrian army.
2. *What do we know about Naaman?*
   Naaman had leprosy.
3. *What did a Hebrew slave girl tell Naaman's wife one day?*
   The Hebrew maid said that God's prophet could heal Naaman.
4. *What did God's prophet Elisha tell Naaman to do?*
   Elisha told Naaman to wash in the Jordan River seven times.
5. *What happened when Naaman had washed in the Jordan?*
   Naaman was cured of his leprosy.
6. *How did God punish Gehazi, Elisha's servant?*
   Gehazi became a leper because he was covetous and a deceiver.

Exercise 1 (True or False)

1. Naaman was a great soldier and he was perfectly well. _____
   (2 Kings 5:1)
2. The little Hebrew maid had faith in God and His prophet. _____
   (2 Kings 5:3)
3. Naaman washed in the Jordan River three times. _____
4. Gehazi became a leper because Naaman visited him. _____
   (2 Kings 5:20-27)

Exercise 2 (Fill in Blanks)

1. Naaman heard of God's _____ through a little slave girl.
2. Naaman had to wash in the _____ River seven times.
3. Naaman was very _____ at Elisha's command.
4. Gehazi found out that secret sins are known by _____.

Something to Think About

1. Are there other instances in the Bible when God used boys or girls to work or speak for Him? See how many you can find.
2. Why do you think the king became so upset when Naaman came to him? Do you think he did not know about Elisha?
3. How did Elisha know about Gehazi's dishonesty?

Memory Verse: Psalm 11:4b.
The Lord's throne is in heaven: his eyes behold...the children of men.

Lesson 21

GOD RESCUES A STARVING CITY
BY FOUR LEPERS

Read: 2 Kings 6, 7

Once again the king of Syria planned to make war against Israel. Each time the Syrian army secretly set up their camp the king of Israel found out where the Syrians were. This troubled the king of Syria. At last the king called his servants together and said, "Will ye not show me which of us is for the king of Israel?" One of the servants said, "None, my lord, O king: but Elisha, the prophet that is in Israel telleth the king of Israel the words that thou speakest in thy bedchamber."

The king said, "Go and spy where he is, that I may send and fetch him." Soon the king was told that Elisha was in Dothan. The king sent a large army with horses and chariots to Dothan. They came by night and surrounded the city.

When Elisha's servant woke up early in the morning he saw the large army of the Syrians. The servant said to Elisha, "Alas, my master! how shall we do?" Elisha answered, "Fear not: for they that be with us are more than they that be with them." Elisha prayed that God would open the eyes of his servant so that he might see. When God opened his eyes, he saw the mountain full of horses and chariots of fire round about Elisha.

Then Elisha prayed that all the Syrians might become blind. The Lord heard his prayer and the Syrians became blind. Elisha told the Syrians they were in the wrong place. He led them to Samaria. When they were within the walls of Samaria, Elisha prayed the Lord to open their eyes. God made them see again and surprise, they were in Samaria.

King Joram was very excited. He thought he could now destroy the Syrian army. But Elisha told the king to feed them and then send them home. The king did as Elisha said, and for a while the Syrians did not trouble Israel.

But this did not last. The king of Syria again made war with Israel and surrounded the city of Samaria. Soon there was a famine in the city. The price of food became so high that only a few could buy it. Animals not fit to eat were used for food. Even a donkey's head was sold for eight pieces of silver. The king blamed Elisha for this trouble. He went out to find Elisha so that he might kill him. When Elisha met the king and the servant, he said, "Thus saith the Lord, Tomorrow about this time shall a measure of fine flour be sold for a shekel (about sixty cents), and two measures of barley for a shekel, in the gate of Samaria. "

The man on whose arm the king leaned said, "Behold, if the Lord would make windows in heaven, might this thing be?" Elisha said, "Behold thou shalt see it with thine eyes, but shalt not eat thereof."

Very early the next morning four lepers were standing outside the gate of Samaria. They said one to another, "Why sit we here until we die?" They decided to go to the camp of the Syrians. They said, "If they save us alive, we shall live; and if they kill us, we shall but die."

When they came to the Syrians' camp they found no man there. The Lord had made the Syrians to hear a noise as of chariots and horses and a great army. The Syrians thought that the king of Israel had hired the kings of the Hittites and Egyptians to help him. The Syrians had left their camp and fled for their life. They had left their animals, their tents, and their food behind.

When the lepers found the food of the Syrians, they ate and drank all they could. They carried the silver and gold, and clothing and hid them. They went from tent to tent and carried away what they found.

After a while, the lepers felt that they were doing wrong. They decided to go to the king and tell him what they had found. When the lepers saw the guard they shouted to him what they had found. The guard quickly told the king.

When the king heard the message of the lepers, he first thought that it was a trick of the Syrians. But the king sent out two men with horses and a chariot. The king said, "Go and see."

The two men found the Syrian camp as the lepers had said. Then the people went out to the Syrian camp. Soon a measure of fine flour was sold for a shekel and two measures of barley for a shekel. The people were hungry and eager to buy food. In their mad rush they trampled to death the king's servant who had charge of the gate. This was the king's servant to whom Elisha had said, "You shall see it with your own eyes, but you shall not eat of it." So God punished unbelief and rescued starving Samaria by four lepers.

QUESTIONS ON LESSON 21

1. *How did king Joram know the secret camping place of the Syrians?*
   Elisha told the king where the Syrians were camped.
2. *For what did Elisha pray when the Syrians came to take him?*
   Elisha prayed that the Syrians might become blind.
3. *What did Elisha do to the Syrians when they became blind?*
   Elisha led the blind Syrians into the city of Samaria.
4. *What happened to the Syrians in Samaria?*
   When Elisha prayed, the Lord opened the eyes of the Syrians.
5. *Why did the king of Israel not destroy the Syrian army?*
   Elisha commanded the king to feed the Syrians and send them home.
6. *How did God provide food for the starving city of Samaria?*
   God used four lepers to find food in the camp of the Syrians.

Exercise 1 (True or False)

1. The king of Syria captured the prophet Elisha. _____.
   (2 Kings 6:18, 19)
2. Elisha allowed king Joram to kill the Syrians. _____ (2 Kings 6:22)
3. When the Syrians again made war, there was a famine in Samaria.
   _____
4. Elisha prophesied there would be food in Samaria. _____

Exercise 2 (Fill in Blanks)

1. Four _____ found the Syrian camp, but the Syrians had
   fled. (2 Kings 7:8-10)
2. The food of the Syrians was sold in _____.
   (2 Kings 7:18)
3. The King's servant saw the food, but did not _____ of it.
   (2 Kings 7:19)
4. The king's servant was trampled under foot and he _____.
   (2 Kings 7:17)

Something to Think About

1. Why could Elisha's servant not see God's army? (See 2 Kings 6:17.)
2. God made the Syrians blind. What about the king's servant?
3. Who brought the glad tidings of food to Samaria first, the prophet
   Elisha or the lepers?
4. Remember that God's promises are His gifts.

Memory Verse: Psalm 68:20a.
He that is our God is the God of salvation.

67

Lesson 22

JONAH, THE DISOBEDIENT PROPHET

Read: Jonah 1-4

After Elisha died, God raised up a prophet named Jonah. God did not send Jonah to teach the people of Israel. God sent him to Nineveh, the capital city of Assyria. Sad to say, the people of Nineveh were very wicked. The Lord said to Jonah "Arise, go to Nineveh, that great city, and cry against it; for their wickedness is come up before me." But Jonah did not want to go to Nineveh. Instead, he went the opposite way. At Joppa he found a ship that was going to Tarshish. He paid the fare and went down into the ship.

In the ship he soon fell fast asleep. After the sailors had loosened the ropes the ship glided along smoothly. But the Lord sent a strong wind and a great storm arose. The ship was in danger. The sailors were afraid and they cried to their gods. The captain came to Jonah and said, "What meanest thou, O sleeper? arise, call upon thy God...that we perish not."

Soon the sailors decided to cast lots to find out whose fault it was that the storm had come upon them. The lot fell upon Jonah. The sailors asked him who he was and what he had done. Jonah said, "I am a Hebrew; and I fear the Lord, the God of heaven, which hath made the sea and the dry land." Jonah also told them that he had fled from the Lord.

The sailors said to Jonah, "What shall we do unto thee, that the sea may be calm unto us?" Jonah said, "Take me up, and cast me forth into the sea; so shall the sea be calm unto you; for I know that for my sake this great tempest is upon you."

The men rowed hard to bring the ship to land, but they could not. They cried to the Lord saying, "We beseech thee, O Lord, let us not perish for this man's life, and lay not upon us innocent blood: for thou, O Lord, hast done as it pleased thee."

Then they threw Jonah overboard. Down into the water he went, and the sea became calm. The sailors knew that this was God's work. When they came to land they offered sacrifices to the Lord and made promises to Him.

But what became of Jonah? He sank down deeper and deeper in the water. But God had prepared a great fish, which opened its mouth and swallowed Jonah alive. In the big fish God kept him safe. Jonah was in the fish for three days and three nights. Surely that gave him time to think things over. He gave thanks to God for saving his life. After the three days God spoke to the fish, and it threw Jonah out upon dry land.

Again the Lord said to Jonah, "Arise, go to Nineveh, that great city, and preach unto it the preaching that I bid thee." This time Jonah obeyed. Walking through the streets of the city he cried, "Yet forty days and Nineveh shall be overthrown." What a stir this message of God brought to the people! They thought of their sins and they trembled with fear. Both rich and poor covered themselves with sackcloth. The king also heard of Jonah's preaching. He arose from his throne. He took off his robe, and put on sackcloth and sat in ashes. The king made a law. In it he commanded everyone to fast, and to pray earnestly to God. He commanded all to turn from their evil ways, and to be truly sorry for their sins.

When God saw what the people did, He did not destroy the city. Jonah was very much displeased about this. He was very angry. He said, "O Lord, was not this my saying, when I was yet in my country? Therefore I fled before unto Tarshish for I know that thou art a gracious God, and merciful, slow to anger, and of great kindness, and repentest thee of the evil."

Jonah prayed that he might die. God said to him, "Doest thou well to be angry?" So Jonah went out of the city. He made himself a little shed and sat down in it.

The Lord caused a vine to grow up over Jonah. It gave him shade from the hot sun. The next day God prepared a worm that bit the stem of the vine so that it withered and died. Then God prepared a strong east wind and the sun beat upon Jonah's head. Jonah felt bad and wished to die.

God said to Jonah, "Thou hast had pity on the gourd, for which thou hast not labored…which came up in a night, and perished in a night. And should I not spare Nineveh…wherein are more that six score thousand persons that cannot discern between their right hand and their left hand; and also much cattle?"

QUESTIONS ON LESSON 22

1. *Where did God send the prophet Jonah?*
   God sent Jonah to preach to the wicked city of Nineveh.
2. *What did Jonah do instead of going to Nineveh?*
   Jonah tried to flee from God in a ship going to Tarshish.
3. *What happened when the ship was out at sea?*
   God sent a great storm, which frightened the sailors and Jonah.
4. *What happened to Jonah after the sailors threw him into the sea?*
   God prepared a great fish that swallowed Jonah.
5. *What happened when Jonah prayed to God?*
   After three days and three nights the fish threw Jonah out on dry land.
6. *What message did Jonah preach in Nineveh after this?*
   Jonah cried to the people, "Yet forty days and Nineveh shall be destroyed."
7. *Why did God not destroy the city of Nineveh?*
   God did not destroy Nineveh because the people repented and prayed.

Exercise 1 (True or False)

1. Jonah obeyed God and went right to Nineveh to preach. _____
2. God punished Jonah by letting him drown in the sea. _____
3. Jonah was thankful to God when he was inside the fish. _____
4. When Jonah preached, the people of Nineveh repented. _____

Exercise 2 (Fill in Blanks)

1. When the sailors cast lots, the lot fell on _____. (Jonah 1:7)
2. Jonah was inside the fish _____ days and _____ nights. (Jonah 1:17)
3. The people of Nineveh believed God and proclaimed a _____. (Jonah 3:5)
4. Jonah said to God. "I knew that thou art a _____ God." (Jonah 4:2)

Something to Think About

1. How often can you find the word "prepared" in the book of Jonah?
2. Did Jesus ever refer to the story of Jonah in his teaching? (See Matthew 12:40.)
3. Do you think Jonah felt sorry for the people of Nineveh?

Memory Verse: Jonah 2:7a.
When my soul fainted within me I remembered the Lord.

Lesson 23

HEZEKIAH, THE GOOD KING

Read: 2 Kings 18, 19, 20; 2 Chronicles 29-32; Isaiah 36-37

When Solomon's son Rehoboam became king, the kingdom of Israel was divided into two kingdoms. The one was called the kingdom of Israel. The other was called the kingdom of Judah. The kingdom of Israel had many wicked kings like Jeroboam and Ahab. The kingdom of Judah had many God-fearing kings. One of these good kings was Hezekiah.

Hezekiah's father, Ahaz, had been the most wicked king of Judah. It may seem strange, but his son Hezekiah was the best king of Judah. Hezekiah became king when he was twenty-five years old.

When Hezekiah had been king for about six years a sad thing happened. The kingdom of Israel was taken captive by the king of Assyria. The Israelites were scattered in a strange land and never returned to their country. God did not bless them anymore because the people would not obey God's Word.

The kingdom of Judah was also very bad. King Ahaz had led the people into sin and closed the temple. But when Hezekiah became king he opened the doors of the temple. The Levites and priests had left the temple, but Hezekiah gathered them all together again to work for the Lord. It took them eight days to clean the temple. The house of God had become filthy and dirty.

When the Levites and priests had finished their work they said to Hezekiah, "We have cleansed all the house of the Lord, and the altar of burnt offering, with all the vessels thereof, and the showbread table, with all the vessels thereof." Hezekiah was glad about this and he offered sacrifices to the Lord. Hezekiah tried very hard to obey the Lord in all things. It was not easy to undo many of the wicked ways of his father Ahaz. The Passover feast had not been held for years. Hezekiah wanted the people to keep the feast as the Israelites had done when Moses was living. He invited a large number to keep the feast, and they decided to stay seven more days.

Hezekiah also asked the people to give one tenth of all their corn and other crops that they raised to the Lord. This was called a *tithe*, and was to be used for the care of the Levites and priests. For a long time these servants of the Lord had been sadly neglected. Hezekiah was glad when the people gave tithes willingly.

After all these things were finished, the king of Assyria made war against Judah. This wicked king captured all the walled cities of Judah and the people were afraid that he would take Jerusalem also. Hezekiah made the walls of Jerusalem stronger and made a large number of darts and spears.

Hezekiah trusted in God. He said to the people: "Be strong and courageous, be not afraid nor dismayed for the king of Assyria, nor for all the multitude that is with him: for there be more with us than with him. With him is an arm of flesh, but with us in the Lord our God to help us, and to fight our battles."

At first, the king of Assyria sent messengers to Hezekiah to talk with him. After that he sent messengers with a letter to Hezekiah. Both times he made fun of Judah and the Lord in whom they trusted. But Hezekiah went into the temple and spread out the letter before the Lord. He prayed for God's help and protection and told the Lord all the wicked things the king had said. Then God sent His prophet Isaiah to Hezekiah. He told him not to fear, for Jerusalem would not be taken. That night an angel of the Lord went out and killed one hundred and eighty-five thousand Assyrian soldiers. The king of Assyria left Jerusalem in shame. Some time later, he was killed by his own sons.

At about this time Hezekiah became very sick. Through the prophet Isaiah the Lord said to him, "Set thine house in order: for thou shalt die, and not live." Then Hezekiah turned his face to the wall and prayed to the Lord with bitter tears.

Before Isaiah had gone out very far the Lord had a message for king Hezekiah. The prophet said, "Thus saith the Lord... I have heard thy prayer, I have seen thy tears: behold, I will heal thee: on the third day thou shalt go up unto the house of the Lord. And I will add unto thy days fifteen years; and I will deliver thee and this city out of the hand of the King of Assyria."

The prophet told Hezekiah to take a lump of figs and put it on his boil and he would recover. As a sign that He would surely heal Hezekiah, God made the sun dial to go ten degrees backward. After this Hezekiah lived fifteen years more, as the Lord had promised.

QUESTIONS ON LESSON 23

1. *How did Hezekiah show that he loved the Lord?*
   Hezekiah cleansed the temple and restored the worship of the true God.
2. *How did Hezekiah provide for the priests and Levites?*
   Hezekiah asked the people to give the priests and Levites a tenth of all that the Lord had given them.
3. *How was Jerusalem spared from being taken by the Assyrians?*
   God heard Hezekiah's prayer and protected Jerusalem.
4. *What did an angel of the Lord do to the Assyrians?*
   In one night an angel of the Lord killed one hundred eighty-five thousand Assyrian soldiers.
5. *What did Hezekiah do when he became very sick?*
   Hezekiah prayed and God added fifteen years to his life.

Exercise 1 (True or False)

1. Hezekiah followed his father in his wicked ways. _____
   (2 Kings 18:3)
2. King Hezekiah commanded his soldiers to clean the temple. _____
   (2 Chron. 29:16)
3. God heard Hezekiah's prayer and protected Jerusalem. _____
   (2 Kings 19:14-20)
4. In one night an angel killed one hundred and eighty-five Assyrians.
   _____ (2 Kings 19:35)

Exercise 2 (Fill in Blanks)

1. Hezekiah opened the doors of the _____. (2 Chron. 29:3)
2. Hezekiah restored the _____ Feast. (2 Chron. 30:1)
3. Hezekiah asked the people to give one _____ to the Lord.
   (2 Chron. 31:4, 5)
4. When the Assyrians threatened, Hezekiah trusted in the _____.
   (2 Kings 19:14, 15)

Something to Think About

1. How do you figure out that Hezekiah was God-fearing when his father was so wicked?
2. What beautiful lessons in prayer are found in 2 Kings 19:14-19 and 20:1-11?

Memory Verse: Psalm 46:1.
God is our refuge and strength, a very present help in trouble.

Lesson 24

GOD'S PROPHETS ISAIAH AND JEREMIAH

Read: Isaiah 6 and 53; Jeremiah 1 and 52

There lived in Israel a great prophet named Isaiah. He was still a young man when king Uzziah died. In that same year the Lord gave Isaiah a wonderful vision. God did this to prepare him for his great work. In the vision the prophet saw the Lord sitting upon a throne. Round about the throne were many angels. They cried to one another saying, "Holy, holy, holy is the Lord God of hosts. The whole earth is full of his glory." Above the throne stood other angels called *seraphim.*

As Isaiah looked he saw the post of the door move at the voice of the one angel. The whole house was filled with smoke. Isaiah was afraid. He cried out, "Woe is me! for I am undone: because I am a man of unclean lips and I dwell in the midst of a people of unclean lips: for mine eyes have seen the King, the Lord of hosts."

One of the seraphim flew to the altar. With a pair of tongs he picked up a live coal from the altar. He laid the coal upon Isaiah's mouth, and said, "Lo, this hath touched thy lips, and thine iniquity is taken away, and thy sin is purged."

Isaiah heard the Lord say, "Whom shall I send, and who will go for us?" Isaiah answered, "Here am I, Lord; send me." God told Isaiah that the people would not obey Isaiah's warnings. Isaiah asked the Lord how long this would continue. The Lord answered, "Until the cities be laid waste without people, and the houses without man, and the land be utterly desolate."

The Lord spoke many hard things about Judah. Yet God promised that after a time a small part of Judah's people would return from their captivity. Isaiah lived many years and spoke many prophecies that are found in the Bible. He foretold many things about the coming Saviour. He tells us so much about the Lord Jesus that his book is sometimes called "The Gospel of the Old Testament."

While Josiah was king over Judah, a baby boy was born in the home of a priest. He also was to become a great prophet. His name was Jeremiah. Being the son of a priest he learned to know God's Word. Like Isaiah, God sent him to warn the people of Judah of their sins.

When Jeremiah was still very young God spoke to him. God told Jeremiah that already before he was born God had chosen him to be a prophet to the nations. Jeremiah said to the Lord, "Ah, Lord God! behold, I cannot speak for I am a child." But the Lord said to him, "Say not, I am a child; for thou shalt go to all that I shall send thee, and whatsoever I command thee, thou shalt speak. Be not afraid of their faces, for I am with thee to deliver thee, saith the Lord."

Then the Lord put forth His hand and touched Jeremiah's mouth. God said to him, "Behold, I have put my words in thy mouth. See, I have set thee over the nations and over the kingdoms, to root out, and to pull down, and to destroy, and to throw down, to build and to plant." What a great work God gave Jeremiah to do!

When Judah had God-fearing kings the people served the Lord. But when these good kings died, the people became wicked again. During the wars with Egypt and other nations many people of Judah were taken captive. God sent Jeremiah to those who were left.

How earnestly Jeremiah warned the people of their wicked way! Oh, how often Jeremiah wept over Judah's sins! Therefore he has been called the "Weeping Prophet." Sometimes the kings would threaten to kill him because of his warnings. At one time his feet were put in the stocks and at another time he was cast into prison.

Finally, the awful punishment that Jeremiah had foretold came upon Judah. It was while Zedekiah was king. God's patience had come to an end. Nebuchadnezzar, king of Babylon, came with a mighty army. He surrounded Jerusalem for two years. At last the city fell. King Zedekiah tried to escape, but he was caught and taken to Babylon. There his sons were killed before his face and then his eyes were put out. That was the last Zedekiah saw. He remained a prisoner for the rest of his life.

Beautiful Jerusalem was destroyed. The people were taken captive to Babylon. Jeremiah stayed in his own land and kept on speaking for the Lord to the people of Judah. He encouraged the people and told them that after seventy years the Lord would bring them back to Jerusalem.

Jeremiah also told the people about the coming Saviour. Truly, Isaiah and Jeremiah were God's great prophets.

QUESTIONS ON LESSON 24

1. *To whom did God send the prophet Isaiah?*
   God sent Isaiah to the people of Judah who had fallen into sin.
2. *What did God show Isaiah in the temple?*
   God showed Isaiah a wonderful vision of angels.
3. *What did Isaiah say when the Lord asked, "Whom shall I send"?*
   Isaiah said, "Here am I, Lord; send me."
4. *What did the king of Babylon do to the Jews?*
   Nebuchadnezzar destroyed the city of Jerusalem, and took the Jews captive to Babylon.
5. *What wonderful news did both Isaiah and Jeremiah bring?*
   Isaiah and Jeremiah told the people about the coming Saviour.

Exercise 1 (True or False)

1. God sent Isaiah to prophesy against Judah. _____ (Isa. 3:8)
2. Isaiah was ready when God prepared him for his work. _____ (Isa. 6:8)
3. Jeremiah did not think he was fit to be God's prophet. _____ (Jer. 1:6)
4. The people of Jerusalem repented and the city was saved. _____ (Jer. 2:12, 13)

Exercise 2 (Fill in Blanks)

1. The angels said, "Holy, holy, holy is the Lord God of _____. (Isa. 6:3)
2. Isaiah said, "Woe is me, ... for I am a man of _____ lips." (Isa. 6:5)
3. Jerusalem was destroyed by the king of _____. (Jer. 52:12)
4. Isaiah and Jeremiah told the people of the coming _____. (Isa. 9-11-53; Jer. 23:5, 6)

Something to Think About

1. Why, do you think, did God make so much of the cleansing of the mouth and lips in preparing the two prophets for their work?
2. How active God's angels are in the work of the Lord! Did you note their obedience and deep reverence for the Lord?
3. God's mercy finally comes to an end with those who continue in sin.

Memory Verse: Isaiah 1:18b.
Though your sins be as scarlet, they shall be as white as snow; though they be red like crimson, they shall be as wool.

Lesson 25

DANIEL AND HIS THREE FRIENDS

Read: Daniel 1-3 and 6

Just before the city of Jerusalem was destroyed, King Nebuchadnezzar sent one of his servants to Jerusalem. He was to bring back some of the Jewish princes to serve in the king's court.

The king commanded his servant to be very careful in selecting these young men. They had to be sons of good families, healthy, handsome, alert and skillful. The king expected that with the proper food and training, in three years they would be well fit for their work.

Among the Jewish princes brought to Babylon were Daniel and three of his friends. The king gave these young men Chaldean names. Daniel he called Belteshazzar. Daniel's three friends he called Shadrach, Meshach, and Abed-nego.

Daniel made up his mind that he was going to obey God also in such things as eating and drinking. He became a good friend to the master of the princes. Daniel asked his master that he and his three friends be allowed to eat vegetables and drink water instead of the king's food. His master did not like to change the king's command. But Daniel asked him to try it for ten days.

The Lord blessed Daniel and his three friends. At the end of ten days the four young men looked healthier and better than the ones who had eaten the king's food. In wisdom and knowledge they were ten times brighter than the wise men of Babylon.

One night king Nebuchadnezzar had a strange dream. The dream had been very real to him. Yet in the morning he could not remember it. When his wise men could not explain nor tell his dream, the king commanded that they should be killed.

Daniel soon heard about the king's dream. He promised the king to tell him the dream and its meaning, if the king would give him time. To this the king agreed. Daniel went home greatly encouraged. He and his three friends prayed and God answered their prayer in a wonderful way. One night God showed Daniel the dream and its meaning. Daniel and his three friends praised and thanked God for His wonderful blessings.

Daniel quickly went to king Nebuchadnezzar and told him that it was impossible for the wise men to tell the king his dream. Daniel said, "But there is a God in heaven that revealeth secrets."

In Daniel 2:24-45 we can read of the king's dream and what God wanted to tell Nebuchadnezzar. How glad the king was when Daniel told him all about his dream! He made Daniel ruler over Babylon and governor over all the wise men. The king placed Daniel's three friends over the affairs of Babylon.

At another time king Nebuchadnezzar made a great golden image of his god. It was about ninety feet high and about nine feet wide, and it could be seen for miles. The king invited all his governors and other high officers to the dedication service. In one part of the program when the herald cried loudly, all the people were to bow down to the king's image. When the music sounded all the people bowed down except Daniel's three friends. They refused to obey the king's command.

As punishment, Daniel's three friends were thrown into a burning furnace. But God protected them. Their clothing was not even singed. God's angel was with them in the furnace. When the king saw how God had protected them, he said, "Blessed be the God of Shadrach, Meshach and Abed-nego."

Some years after this Babylon had a king named Darius. This king gave Daniel a very high office. Some of the lower rulers became very jealous. They knew that Daniel was a God-fearing man.

These officers asked the king to make a law that anyone who would ask a favour of any god or man, except the king, should be thrown into the den of lions. Daniel prayed before his open window three times every day. When the officers saw this, they told the king. Darius liked Daniel very much but he had to be true to his decree, because that was the law of his country.

Daniel was cast into the lion's den but God kept the lions' mouths shut so they did him no harm. How happy Darius was that God spared Daniel! But he was angry with the other officers. He commanded his men to take Daniel out and to cast the jealous officers into the lions' den. The lions destroyed them in a hurry. Then Darius made a decree that all men should fear and tremble before the God of Daniel.

QUESTIONS ON LESSON 25

1. *Why did the king bring Daniel and his three friends to the palace?*
   Daniel and his friends were to be Nebuchadnezzar's officers.
2. *How did the Lord bless Daniel before King Nebuchadnezzar?*
   God showed Daniel the king's dream and its meaning.
3. *Why were Shadrach, Meshach and Abed-nego thrown into the fiery furnace?*
   Daniel's three friends refused to bow down before the king's image.
4. *How were the three young men saved?*
   God's angel protected them so that the fire did not hurt them.
5. *How did Daniel show that he was not afraid of King Darius?*
   Daniel prayed three times each day in spite of the king's decree.
6. *How did the Lord protect Daniel in the den?*
   God kept the lions' mouths shut so that they could not hurt Daniel.

Exercise 1 (True or False)

1. Daniel and his three friends were brought to Babylon. _____ (Dan. 1:1-7)
2. Daniel did not dare to refuse the king's command. _____ (Dan. 1:8)
3. Daniel's friends soon died in the fiery furnace. _____ (Dan. 3:27, 28)
4. Darius was glad God had saved Daniel from the lions. _____ (Dan. 6:23)

Exercise 2 (Fill in Blanks)

1. Daniel made known the king's _____ and its meaning. (Dan. 2:36-45)
2. Nebuchadnezzar made a great _____. (Dan. 3:1)
3. Daniel's three friends were cast into a fiery _____. (Dan. 3:21)
4. God's angel kept the lions' _____ _____ so they could not hurt Daniel. (Dan. 6:22)

Something to Think About

1. Do young people usually find it easier to obey God away from home?
2. Why did Daniel's friends not give in? After all, "everybody else was doing it." (Dan. 3:17)
3. Why do you think Daniel prayed before the open window? Was he inviting trouble, or was there another reason? (Dan. 6:10)

Memory Verse: Matthew 10:32.
Whosoever therefore shall confess me before men,
him will I confess before my Father which is in heaven.

Lesson 26

DANIEL BEFORE NEBUCHADNEZZAR
AND BELSHAZZAR

Read: Daniel 4 and 5

One day King Nebuchadnezzar was resting in his beautiful palace. A dream came to him that made him very much afraid. He called in all his wise men to explain his dream but they could not tell its meaning. Daniel was also asked to come before the king. Nebuchadnezzar was eager to tell him the dream. In his dream the king saw a large tree with beautiful leaves and much fruit. The top of it reached to heaven. The tree could be seen throughout all the earth. The animals rested in its shade and the birds made nests in its branches.

The king also saw a messenger coming down from heaven. The messenger cried aloud, "Hew down that tree, and cut off his branches, shake off his leaves, and scatter his fruit: let the beasts get away from under it, and the fowls from his branches. Nevertheless, leave the stump of his roots in the earth, even with a band of iron and brass, in the tender grass of the field; and let it be wet with the dew of heaven, and let his portion be with the beasts in the grass of the earth; let his heart be changed from man's and let a beast's heart be given unto him; and let seven times pass over it."

The messenger said that this was to happen so that all people might know that the most high God is ruler over all men and that He gives the kingdom to whom He desires.

Daniel told Nebuchadnezzar that the tree represented the king himself. He told the king that he would be driven from men and live with the beasts of the field. For seven years he would eat grass like oxen. His body would be wet with the dew of heaven until he would know that the most high God rules over all men and gives the kingdom to whomsoever He wills. After that God would give him his kingdom back again.

About one year after this the king was walking in his palace. In his pride he said, "Is this not great Babylon, that I have built?" Then a voice from heaven said, "O king Nebuchadnezzar, to thee it is spoken; The kingdom is departed from thee." The same hour the king became wild and his reason left him. He was driven into the fields. He ate grass like the oxen. His body became wet with the dew. His hair grew like eagles' feathers and his nails like birds' claws.

At the end of seven years the king looked up to heaven. His understanding came back again, and he praised the most high God. Then Nebuchadnezzar came back to his kingdom again to rule. He had learned to bow before God.

After Nebuchadnezzar died, Belshazzar became king of Babylon. This king did not worship God. One day Belshazzar made a great feast and invited a thousand of his great men to come to the palace. While they were drinking wine the king commanded his servants to bring the golden and silver dishes Nebuchadnezzar had stolen out of the temple in Jerusalem. The wicked king and his men drank wine from the vessels of the temple. Then they praised their own heathen gods.

As they were drinking, the fingers of a man's hand appeared on the wall. The fingers were writing an unknown language. When Belshazzar saw it he promised his wise men great rewards if they could read the writing. But they could not read it. Then the queen urged the frightened king to call for Daniel.

Then Daniel was brought in before king Belshazzar. The king promised Daniel great rewards if he could explain the writing.

Daniel told the king to keep his rewards, or to give them to someone else. Daniel said, "I will read the writing unto the king." He told the king how the Lord God had made King Nebuchadnezzar great and had blessed him. He also told the king how God had punished Nebuchadnezzar when he had become proud, until he knew that God ruled over all men.

Daniel said to King Belshazzar, "And thou his son, O Belshazzar, hast not humbled thine heart, though thou knewest all this; but hast lifted up thyself against the God of heaven." Daniel reminded the king of his wickedness in using the vessels of God's house and praising dead idols.

Then Daniel read the writing: "Mene, Mene, Tekel, Upharsin." He told the king that it meant: "God hath numbered thy kingdom and finished it. Thou art weighed in the balances and art found wanting. Thy kingdom is divided, and given to the Medes and Persians."

Then the king commanded to clothe Daniel with scarlet and to give him his reward. In that same night Belshazzar was killed. Thus ended the life of a wicked king.

QUESTIONS ON LESSON 26

1. *How did God show Daniel's great wisdom?*
   Daniel was able to explain Nebuchadnezzar's dream.
2. *Why did God send the strange dream to Nebuchadnezzar?*
   God wanted to teach Nebuchadnezzar that He is Ruler over all things.
3. *How did God take away King Nebuchadnezzar's pride?*
   God caused Nebuchadnezzar to lose his mind and live like an animal for seven years.
4. *What happened while wicked King Belshazzar was feasting in his palace?*
   God sent the fingers of a man's hand to write on the wall.
5. *Whom did the king call to explain the writing?*
   Belshazzar asked Daniel to tell the meaning of the writing.
6. *What happened to Belshazzar that same night?*
   Belshazzar was killed and his kingdom was given to others.

Exercise 1 (True or False)

1. The wise men of Nebuchadnezzar explained his strange dream.
   _____
2. Daniel did not like to tell the king the meaning of his dream. _____
   (Dan. 4:19)
3. Daniel told the king not to pay any attention to his dream. _____
   (Dan. 4:27)
4. After one year Nebuchadnezzar's dream came true. _____
   (Dan. 4:29)

Exercise 2 (Fill in Blanks)

1. Nebuchadnezzar said, "Is not this great _____ that I have built? (Dan. 4:30)
2. Nebuchadnezzar had to eat grass like the _____.
   (Dan. 4:33)
3. Belshazzar saw the fingers of a man's hand writing on the _____.
   (Dan. 5:5)
4. "In that night was Belshazzar the king _____.
   (Dan. 5:30)

Something to Think About

1. Only a few people can stand to be rich and highly honoured.
2. Great kings may become mighty, but God is Almighty.
3. "Pride cometh before destruction and a haughty spirit before a fall."

Memory Verse: Psalm 25:14a.
The secret of the Lord is with them that fear him.

Lesson 27

QUEEN ESTHER

Read: The Book of Esther

After Darius died, his son Ahasuerus became king of Persia. The capital of the kingdom was in Shushan.

King Ahasuerus invited all the people of Shushan to a great feast. On the seventh day of the feast, when the king had drunk too much wine, he did a foolish thing. He commanded his servants to bring in Queen Vashti to show all the men her beauty. The queen knew this was wrong and refused to come. This made the king very angry. Upon advice of his great men he put Queen Vashti away.

After some time the king sent for all the beautiful girls of his kingdom. Of these he wanted to choose a queen in Vashti's place. Among these girls was a young Jewish girl named Esther who had been brought up by her cousin Mordecai. The king chose Esther to be the new queen.

One day Mordecai discovered that two wicked men wanted to kill the king. He warned Esther about this. Both men were found guilty and were hanged. The king made a record of this in his books.

King Ahasuerus chose a man named Haman to rule over the other princes. All the king's servants bowed before him according to the king's command. But Mordecai refused to bow before him. This made Haman so angry that he wanted to kill Mordecai. When Haman found out that Mordecai was a Jew he planned to kill all the Jews. The king, not knowing that this was the nation to which queen Esther belonged, gave Haman permission to write to all the rulers that all the Jews in the kingdom should be killed in one day.

When Mordecai heard about all this he tore his clothes, and put on sackcloth. Esther sent a servant to Mordecai to ask what troubled him. Mordecai sent a copy of Haman's decree to Esther, and asked her to do everything possible to save the Jews. Esther sent word back to Mordecai saying that it was dangerous to go to the king without being called. Unless the king would hold out his golden sceptre, it would mean certain death.

Esther asked Mordecai to tell all the Jews in Shushan to fast for her. She and her maidens would fast also. Then she would go to the king. She said, "If I perish, I perish."

After three days Esther went in to the king. When the king saw her he held out his golden sceptre. The king asked her, "What is thy request?" Esther answered, "Let the king and Haman come this day unto the banquet that I have prepared for him."

The king and Haman came to Esther's banquet. When the king asked Esther what she desired she asked that the king and Haman come to her banquet again the next day. Haman felt very proud and happy. He went home to tell his friends about it. But when Haman saw Mordecai, and Mordecai did not bow to him, Haman was angry. He told his wife about Mordecai. She suggested making a high gallows on which to hang Mordecai. Haman agreed to this and made the gallows.

That night the king could not sleep. He called a man to read the book of records of his kingdom. In it he found that Mordecai had saved the king from being killed by two wicked men. He asked his servant what reward Mordecai had received for this. The servant said, "There is nothing done for him."

Then the king called Haman. He said to him, "What shall be done unto the man whom the king delighteth to honour?" Haman thought the king was talking about him because the king favoured him. Haman told the king that the man whom the king wanted to honour should be dressed in royal clothing, should wear the royal crown, and ride on the king's horse through the city.

The king told Haman to do all this to Mordecai. Then Haman had to dress Mordecai in the king's clothes and lead him on horseback through the city.

While Haman was telling his wife about Mordecai, the king's servant came to take him to Esther's banquet. At the banquet the king asked Esther for her request. Esther said, "If I have found favor in thy sight, O king, and if it please the king, let my life be given me at my petition, and my people at my request: for we are sold, I and my people, to be destroyed."

The king said, "Who is he, and where is he, that durst presume in his heart to do so?" Esther answered, "The enemy is this wicked Haman." The king commanded that Haman should be hanged on the gallows, which he had prepared for Mordecai.

Esther asked the king that all the Jews might not be destroyed. The king gladly did this. Then two days were set apart for the Jews to remember God's wonderful care of His people.

QUESTIONS ON LESSON 27

1. *Why did Ahasuerus put away queen Vashti?*
   Vashti would not obey the king's sinful command.
2. *Whom did King Ahasuerus choose to be queen in Vashti's place?*
   The king chose Esther, a beautiful Jewish girl, to be his queen.
3. *What wicked plan did Haman place before the king?*
   Haman asked the king that all the Jews be destroyed.
4. *Why did King Ahasuerus honour Mordecai?*
   Mordecai had saved the king's life.
5. *What favour did Esther ask of the king?*
   Esther asked the king and Haman to come to her banquet.
6. *What did Esther tell the king at the banquet?*
   Esther told the king that Haman planned to destroy her and her people.
7. *How did the king punish Haman?*
   Haman was hanged on the gallows, which he had made for Mordecai.

Exercise 1 (True or False)

1. Vashti obeyed king Ahasuerus in all things._____ (Esther 1:12)
2. Haman placed Mordecai over all the princes. _____ (Esther 3:1)
3. Haman planned to destroy all the Jews. _____ (Esther 3:8)
4. Esther at first was afraid to go to the king. _____ (Esther 4:10-14)

Exercise 2 (Fill in Blanks)

1. The king chose _____ to be his queen. (Esther 2:17)
2. The king held out his _____ to Esther. (Esther 5:2)
3. Esther told the king about _____ wicked plan. (Esther 7:1-6)
4. Haman was hung on the gallows he planned for _____. (Esther 7:10)

Something to Think About

1. God's people are to Him as the apple of His eye.
2. We had better be careful for whom we build a gallows.

Memory Verse: Proverbs 15:29.
The Lord is far from the wicked: but he heareth the prayer of the righteous.

Lesson 28

THE JEWS RETURN TO JERUSALEM

Read: Ezra and Nehemiah

God had promised the Jews through His prophet Jeremiah, that after seventy years they would return to Jerusalem. These seventy years were nearly over. The prophet Isaiah had prophesied years ago that God would use a man named Cyrus to bring the Jews back to their own land. Now this Cyrus was king of Persia.

When Cyrus became king, God put into his heart a desire to help the Jews return to Jerusalem. Cyrus even offered to help them rebuild the temple, which had been destroyed. The king made a writing in which he gave all the Jews permission to go back to Jerusalem. How happy the Jews were when they read the writing of the king! With glad hearts about fifty thousand people made the journey to Jerusalem.

When the people came to Jerusalem they found the city in ruins. It had been so ever since King Nebuchadnezzar had burned it to the ground, seventy years ago. Not a single house was left standing. So they had to live in tents until houses could be built.

King Cyrus gave back to the Jews all the golden and silver platters, which King Nebuchadnezzar had taken out of the temple of Jerusalem. When the people had lived in Jerusalem one year and their homes were built, they began to build the temple. What a happy day it must have been for the Jews to lay the foundation for the new house of God! They praised the Lord and sang of the great mercies of the Lord.

After this, God provided a wonderful teacher of the Word of God for the Jews who had returned to Jerusalem. His name was Ezra. Ezra was a Jew living in Persia. He asked the king to let him go to Jerusalem to teach the people the things of God's Word. The king was willing to let him go. He also gave permission to other Jews to go with him. The king gave him a fine present of gold and silver, and gold and silver dishes. All this was to be an offering for the Lord.

Before starting on the long journey Ezra held a prayer service with those who were with him. They asked God to forgive all their wrongdoing and to give them a safe journey.

Ezra came to Jerusalem with about six thousand people. They brought the gold and the silver to the temple, and offered sacrifices to the Lord. After this, some of the princes told Ezra that certain Jews had married heathen wives. This was forbidden by God. Ezra was so troubled about this that he tore his clothes and plucked his hair out of his head and beard. Then he prayed to the Lord. While he prayed, a large crowd of people came to see him. They confessed their sin and promised to put their heathen wives away.

At this time there lived in Persia a rich Jew named Nehemiah. He was the cupbearer to the king. The Lord put into his heart a desire to help the Jews in far off Jerusalem. Like Ezra, he prayed about this.

After asking God for advice, Nehemiah went to the king to ask for permission to help his people. God made the king willing to let him go. The king sent letters to all the governors of the land through which Nehemiah would have to travel. He also asked them to give Nehemiah lumber to build the walls of Jerusalem.

When Nehemiah came to Jerusalem, he told the people he had come to help them. They immediately began to work, clearing up the rubbish and rebuilding the walls. But the enemies made it hard for the Jews to work. First, they laughed at them, and then they threatened to destroy them. But Nehemiah was strong and firm. He told the workers to have their swords by their sides while they worked so they could defend themselves. Steadily the building of the walls went on until in fifty-two days the walls were completed. Nehemiah and the people had worked hard. The Lord had blessed their work.

After this, Nehemiah called all the people together for a feast day. Ezra read the Word of God for them and others helped to explain it to the people. Then they returned to their homes for a happy holiday.

During this time there lived a prophet whose name was Malachi. He wrote the last book of the Old Testament. In it he tells us of Jesus the Saviour as the Sun of righteousness who would arise with healing in his wings. He also tells us of the coming of John the Baptist who would come as the messenger of the Christ. Malachi urged the people to turn to the Lord, to serve and worship Him, and to give their tithes to the Lord.

QUESTIONS ON LESSON 28

1. *How long were the Jews in captivity in Babylon?*
   The Jews stayed in Babylon for seventy years.
2. *What great king did God raise up to allow the Jews to return?*
   God raised up King Cyrus to help the Jews.
3. *Why did God send Ezra to Jerusalem?*
   God sent Ezra to Jerusalem to teach the people the Word of God.
4. *For what great work did God send Nehemiah to Jerusalem?*
   God sent Nehemiah to help rebuild the walls of Jerusalem.
5. *What did Nehemiah do after the walls were completed?*
   Nehemiah called all the people together for a feast day.
6. *What did Malachi call the Saviour in the last book of the Old Testament?*
   Malachi called the Saviour the Sun of Righteousness.

Exercise 1 (True or False)

1. The Jews never returned to Jerusalem again. _____ (Ezra 2)
2. God used King Cyrus to help the Jews return. _____ (Ezra 1)
3. King Cyrus restored all the golden and silver vessels to the Jews.
   _____ (Ezra 1:11)
4. Nehemiah did not care to help the Jews. _____ (Neh. 1)

Exercise 2 (Fill in Blanks)

1. The Jews remained in captivity _____ years.
   (2 Chron. 36:21)
2. When Ezra was afraid, he _____ to God for help.
   (Ezra 8:23)
3. Nehemiah _____ to God before he spoke to the king.
   (Neh. 2:4)
4. Malachi tells of the Saviour as "the _____ of Righteousness."
   (Mal. 2)

Something to Think About

1. God is faithful to every promise He makes.
2. The hearts of great men and kings are in God's hand.
3. We ought to note the important place of prayer and confession of sin in our lesson.

Memory Verse: Psalm 126:3.
The Lord hath done great things for us; whereof we are glad.